ABOUT THE AUTHOR

J.M. Kearns, PhD, is a writer of fiction and non-fiction who has at various times been a philosopher of perception, a crisis counselor and a music journalist. He brings to relationship books the unusual combination of a philosopher's analytical mind and a novelist's insight into emotions. His book *Why Mr. Right Can't Find You* (2007–8) has been embraced by readers and the press on both sides of the Atlantic and featured on *Oprah & Friends* and in *OK!* Magazine, *Glamour*, *Cosmopolitan-UK*, *Maclean's*, *The Toronto Star*, and many others. Since then two more Kearns books have been published to critical praise. His novel *ex-Cottagers in Love* (2008) is a dark-humored exploration of a mid-life crisis, and his second relationship book, *Better Love Next Time* (2009), tackles the problem of how to heal your romantic soul and decode the lessons of the past. J.M. Kearns grew up near Toronto, Canada, and now lives in Cape May, New Jersey, with his partner Debra.

For more on Kearns and his writings, please visit
www.jmkearns.com

PRAISE FOR J.M. KEARNS' WRITING

Why Mr. Right Can't Find You:

"If you've been on the lookout for ages but still haven't found The One, this is for you . . . you'll be in the arms of your true love in no time!"

— *OK!* Magazine

"Practical, encouraging and . . . optimistic . . . Kearns gently undermines the conventions and insecurities that keep [women] from actively and effectively seeking a mate, including self-defeating myths ("Serious relationships never begin in bars") and media-inspired body-image issues . . . Personal anecdotes round out this thorough, thoughtful and entirely upbeat dating guide."

— *Publishers Weekly*

"I review self-help books for a living and this is the best self-help book I've ever read."

— Julia McKinnell, Contributing editor, *Maclean's*

"'I'm bringing the good news from the male side of the trenches,' said J.M. Kearns . . . 'To set the record straight and defend the much-maligned male gender, who I think have been distorted in the self-help literature for years.' Mr. Kearns said . . . men [have been] presented in . . . dating literature as a homogeneous block to be tricked, decoded and subdued by women. 'If you worry about what most men are looking for, you'll go wrong,' he said. These books tell women they must act in accordance with a prescribed set of rules that has nothing to do with how men actually think."

— *Globe and Mail*

"Unlike most such books, *Why Mr. Right Can't Find You* is funny, inspiring and quite practical. A new book aimed specifically at successful, real single women, it may be just the thing you need to find Mr. Right-for-you. And it's been known to help a few men find their Ms. Right."
— Carolyn Cooke in *The Now Newspaper*

"J.M. Kearns in his excellent new book *Why Mr. Right Can't Find You,* . . . unlike other self-helps for the single woman, starts with the premise that there is nothing wrong with you. You do not need to be 'fixed'. Kearns . . . has a Ph.D. in philosophy and has worked as a crisis counsellor . . . Whereas other how-tos portray men as unknowable aliens interested only in hard-to-get women, Kearns has a different take. A lot of men . . . he says, want a meaningful relationship. 'Contrary to the dating books,' he writes, 'if you get into a conversation with the right man you won't have a problem knowing what to say!'"
— Julia McKinnell, *Maclean's*

Better Love Next Time:

"Read it, people. J.M. Kearns's new book called *Better Love Next Time* . . . The book's main premise is that people often repeat the same mistakes in successive relationships, but if you can diagnose what really went wrong with your exes, you can have better relationships in the future."
— Erin Meanley, *Glamour.com*

"I laughed a bit and contemplated my past relationships right along with what J.M. Kearns was saying. I felt like I was having a discussion with him but I didn't need to speak. This book was so well written; I finished it with a smile on my face and a heart full of hope."
— *The Book Club Queen*

"For anyone who is nursing a broken heart or just has bad luck in love, *Better Love Next Time* is a great read. Not only does it allow you to learn about yourself, it encourages you to grow and get yourself ready for the love of your life!"

— *CollegeCandy.com*

". . . aimed at getting you back in the game and emerging a winner . . . Working from the principle that past relationships contain the coded map that will lead to successful love, Kearns offers advice on how to unlock the code and stop making the same mistakes."

— *The National Post*

"Self-help books often make me skittish—but not this one. Kearns's advice is sound and good: he tells us to look inward, to be honest with ourselves, to stay the course. A chapter called How Good Matches Go Bad is, alone, worth the book's price . . . He says our demons will invariably rise up and try to disrupt . . . It's important to learn to step back when you sense trouble 'and ask yourself, who is talking here?' Are there old grudges in play? Old hurts stinging? False lessons echoing that have nothing to do with the two of you?"

— Susan Schwartz, *Montreal Gazette*

READERS SPEAK ABOUT

Why Mr. Right Can't Find You:

"The book of hope. I followed its advice straight to a great new man I met, and now I'm happily married to him!"

— Olivia D.

"This book makes you look at relationships from a completely different perspective. I approached someone through an avenue I had never thought of before (because Kearns helped me to see opportunities, and empowered me to do something about it) and we have been dating ever since. The difference about this relationship is that I didn't approach it with a sense of lack or deficiency. This is truly a new day and a new way for me!"

— Lorraine L.

"This book doesn't even deserve to be lumped in with all the other "Self Help" stuff: it's better than that. I was shocked to find an intelligent discussion of something people almost never speak intelligently about—preferring instead to believe in some pie-in-the-sky fantasy at the exact moment they're planning a life! I brought this book to my boyfriend when we'd only been going out a few weeks: we read it together, talked about it, went on a road trip to test it out, and basically used it as a roadmap to find true compatibility . . . at the same time we were falling in love. I highly recommend it for couples, not just singles, because it jump-starts those conversations and questions you need to figure out before you get all emotional and sappy. We now know things about each other we'd never thought to ask ourselves. Oddly enough, after you figure out you really can be best friends and great partners, all that dreamy love stuff is much deeper and more rewarding. Great book—and the little vignettes make it hilarious, too."

— Marguerite P.

shopping for mr. right

shopping for mr. right

how to choose the right guy and get the most out of him

J.M. Kearns

John Wiley & Sons Canada, Ltd.

Library and Archives Canada Cataloguing in Publication

Kearns, J. M. (J. Michael)
    Shopping for Mr. Right : how to choose the right one and get the most out of him / J.M. Kearns.

Issued also in electronic formats.

ISBN 978-0-470-96414-9

    1. Mate selection. 2. Man-woman relationships. I. Title.

HQ801.K415 2010   646.7'7   C2010-905827-5

ISBN (ebk): 978-0-470-96501-6, 978-0-470-96503-0, 978-0-470-96502-3

Production Credits
Cover design: Ian Koo
Interior design & layout: Adrian So
Author photo: Debra Donahue
Printer: Friesens Printing Ltd.

Editorial Credits
Managing Editor: Alison Maclean
Production Editor: Pauline Ricablanca

John Wiley & Sons Canada, Ltd.
6045 Freemont Blvd.
Mississauga, Ontario
L5R 4J3

Printed in Canada

1 2 3 4 5 FP 15 14 13 12 11

ENVIRONMENTAL BENEFITS STATEMENT

John Wiley & Sons - Canada saved the following resources by printing the pages of this book on chlorine free paper made with 100% post-consumer waste.

TREES	WATER	SOLID WASTE	GREENHOUSE GASES
55	25,282	1,535	5,249
FULLY GROWN	GALLONS	POUNDS	POUNDS

Calculations based on research by Environmental Defense and the Paper Task Force.
Manufactured at Friesens Corporation

contents

INTRODUCTION   1

PART ONE: The nature of the man-beast   **11**

1. Testosterone is your friend   13
2. The male ego   21
3. But really now, do men talk about their feelings?   33
4. Yeah, but men don't like to talk about *relationships*, right?   39
5. Are men aliens from Mars?   45

PART TWO: Shopping criteria   **51**

6. Shopping for status   53
7. Old and improved   59
8. Shopping for someone who is shopping for you   65
9. Portray the man you seek   69
10. Love you can afford   77

PART THREE: Let's shop!   **85**

11. Shop, and always shop   87
12. Imagine the shopping situation he's in and cater to it   91
13. The Sleeping Beauty Syndrome   101
14. Can you be the aggressor?   107
15. Proxy shopping   115

PART FOUR: Shopping for Mr. Right online   **121**

16. This time it's personals   123

17. The two searches that reveal if a dating site is for you   129

18. How to do a custom search for your custom man   135

19. The best shoppers advertise too   141

20. The contact barrier   147

21. Other sites, other prices   153

22. Can Facebook get you to Mr. Right?   163

23. What about long-distance love? My own story   171

24. From virtual to real   177

PART FIVE: The trial period—and beyond   **181**

25. Testing love by trying love   183

26. Your own love lab   189

27. If you fall in love, does that prove
you're with the right guy?   201

28. Why the big rush?   209

29. Why does a guy suddenly disappear
when things were going so well?   215

30. Should you judge a man by what he is now,
or by what he could be?   219

31. If you have fights, does that mean
it's not going to work out?   223

32. Shopping addiction and getting exclusive   227

33. How Cupid tries to cheat you
out of happiness with Mr. Right   231

Acknowledgments   **237**

introduction

$\mathcal{I}$came late to shopping. And reluctantly. In fact, as I'll tell in a minute, I had to be dragged kicking and screaming to its delights.

But I have had my awakening, my blinding light on the road to Macy's.

I now know that shopping is the answer, the only answer.

I wrote two relationship books and then I stood back to survey the results. They were full of good thoughts, on why Mr. Right can't find you and on how to heal your romantic soul so you can achieve a better love next time. They covered their ground well.

But when I looked around, something was still wrong. *Why Mr. Right Can't Find You* was a bestseller on Amazon, but apparently that wasn't enough.

The divorce rate hadn't gone down.

There were still way too many women in need of a partner. And men feeling the same . . .

And I hadn't been on *Oprah*. This just wouldn't do.

That's when it hit me, we still haven't brought the right talent to bear on the challenge of finding true love. How do you solve a problem in life? Look for something you already know how to do that will work in this situation. Mate finding doesn't have to be a daunting, confusing riddle. Turn your full, fearsome prowess on it. Approach it as shopping.

Great challenges call for great remedies.

And the first challenge is men. The whole hairy throng of them. When you set out to find true love, you aren't faced with Mr. Right. You don't need to understand him yet. You need to find your way to him, but he lies somewhere in that vast tribe of dudes.

So we'll start with this question: What are men all about?

They are fine creatures, admittedly. They have big muscles and fascinating facial hair and when they dance with you, their eyes gleam and their pants bulge. They come in all shapes and sizes, one is bound to fit you.

So what's the problem?

It's that men are also a major puzzle.

They have this thing called testosterone. It makes them sexy, and good at shoveling snow, but it also makes them fight—sometimes over the wrong things—and take reckless chances. Men are broad-chested and brave; so why are so many of them afraid? Or easily hurt? Does testosterone even work anymore? It has fallen on hard times, as men are increasingly stuck in a world where it doesn't really fit, a world of offices and softwares and two-earner couples. So it's been driven off the main road into a mostly symbolic alley, where boys and men play video games and watch football and dream of Ultimate Fighting. What is a woman to make of this; what should she hope for in her man's hormonal brew?

Then there's that famous male ego. Along with testosterone, it has earned a bad reputation.

All this adds up to the cliché that men are from Mars.[1] Plus a bunch of stereotypes about how men can't communicate emotionally, can't commit, are only looking for sex, all that. Are they true? Is it best to think of men as aliens?

But wait, aren't a lot of men good brothers, good fathers, good husbands, ready to die for the ones they love?

So why is it so hard to nab a good one?

Because it *is* hard.

And that's the second challenge. Even when you free men from the false charges, this choosing-a-mate stuff isn't that simple. You have to sift through the different types of guy and know which one suits you. You have to see beyond the packaging to the quality within. Part of the problem is that the things that attract you during the fun, getting-it-on phase aren't necessarily the things you're going to want down the line. Danger? Sexy. Reliability? Useful. And when you're in love, you can be blinded to the real person who is in front of you.

Love itself—romantic love—is in many ways a myth, fueled by a multi-million-dollar industry hawking flowers and movies and travel and . . . weddings. It sells the idea that perfect bliss lasts forever. The problem is, it doesn't. If you choose the right person, it gets replaced by something richer, deeper, and better. *If* you pull that off. So your job when you're picking a man is to see past the dizzy infatuation of now, into the future: to see what this guy will be like and how the two of you will interact when things get more real. That's right—you need to time travel, to peer into the long term.

You don't know *exactly* what you're looking for until you find it—and even then you may not know for quite a while. So picking the

---

1. I'm referring to the simplistic idea that is part of our culture, not the book that spawned it, which is more nuanced.

right partner and then closing the deal with him is no mean feat. You need to make fine distinctions; you need to be skeptical at times and yet able to accept value when you see it. Even unexpected, surprising value. You need to boldly put yourself forward and say who you are. It calls for persistence and energy and curiosity. You have to be proactive, and it takes courage and yes, aggression.

But, this all sounds familiar. Isn't there another activity that requires a person to be discerning, selective, proactive, and the rest? And aren't you already good at it?

Yes, by god there is, and you are.

Which brings us back to shopping. And the good news is, the female brain is wired for shopping. Through the ages, this sacred skill has been handed down through your tribe by your mothers and their mothers' mothers. Once it was women clad in skins, kneeling in the forest to tell the brownish knobby plant that cures headache from the brownish knobby plant that kills you. The talent of the gatherer. Now it's the modern woman who knows how to shop for anything from a house to a smartphone to the perfect pair of heels.

So you have this excellent skill set, just waiting to be applied to the most important "purchase" of your life. And that's what I'm saying in this book; this is the way to bring home a fabulous partner.

When you think about mate finding as shopping, lots of light bulbs go on:

- **In some ways, the quest for a partner is like regular shopping.** For example, sometimes you make the mistake of buying the dress that is all the rage instead of the one that looks good on you. Same thing happens with men: I call it buying for status, and Chapter 6 tells why it doesn't lead to the guy you really want. Another example: If you wait till you really need a gift for your sister, it's much harder to find it. It's better to be on the lookout all the time. That's equally true of men. Third, a more mystic point. In a weird way, shopping is an interaction between the person you are now and the person you want to be. So is the search for a partner.

- **In other ways, mate finding is a different form of shopping, unique to itself.** For example, it's shopping for someone who's shopping for you, something a coat or a lamp can't do. I call this *reciprocal shopping* and it brings with it a huge potential advantage, on which success turns. Budget is another example. In regular shopping it pretty much means, get as much as you can for the money you can afford. I'll show that it has a totally different meaning when it comes to a partner. A third case in point: most products we buy are static; they aren't going to change or grow. But the deepest love connects with the other person's potential, not just their actuality, and helps it be born.

- **Most remarkably, mate finding and shopping have converged in recent times, have morphed into the *very same* activity.** Looking for a man on a dating site is pretty much like looking for a book on Amazon, only the search engine is more powerful. I devote a section to the online route to love, which has unprecedented power to advance your quest.

No matter what form it takes, shopping is the right idea at the right time. Because it isn't just something you're naturally equipped for, practiced at, and liable to be intrepid about.

Shopping—on a good day in the right store with enough moolah—is also a blast.

Not that I always understood this. When I was fifteen my parents took me and my older sister to New York City. They went off on their own and left me with her. And what did she want to do? She wanted to shop. Now, my sister was and is a very good shopper. And that was my nightmare, because I not only wasn't good at it, I just didn't get it. Most of my clothes up till then had been bought by my mother, and when I tried occasionally to buy something for myself, I found the whole process confusing and somehow embarrassing. So I only ventured into stores when I had a specific thing I wanted, and then I spent as little time there as possible. What shopping meant to my sister was something completely different. It was more about the journey than the destination. I didn't understand it, or how she could possibly enjoy it.

I was a lanky nerd who loved folk-rock songs, and what I wanted to do was walk the streets of this colossal city, maybe find a club in the Village with some live music, and most of all sit at a sidewalk table and try for a Bob Dylan sighting. Oh, and watch New York women go by.

So I didn't want to be with my sister, but most of all I didn't want to be her companion and assistant as she shopped.

"What are you looking for today?" I said as we hit the street.

"Oh, I don't know, maybe a raincoat, maybe a blouse."

But I knew it wasn't true. She wanted everything in the city; she wanted to *look* at everything, that is, and then as a bonus she might occasionally make a purchase. We invaded a major department store, maybe it was Saks. I tried to steer her toward some raincoats I saw in the corner; we were sailing in the right direction—and then she saw a dress off to starboard, maybe a mile away. *No, no,* I muttered, *that wasn't on the list!* But it was useless. She had changed course.

While she explored the store, I trained my eyes on the same things she looked at, but I felt like I was blind. She knew five kinds of lapel, seven kinds of waistline, and seventeen styles of belt buckle. She knew hundreds of subtle variations of purse, and she had *feelings* about each of them. Now and then she would ask me if I liked something, but my answer, which was usually based on a coin toss in my head, had no effect on her process. After two hours I was physically exhausted and she had bought one scarf. Then I saw the cosmetics counter ahead, and I knew I was doomed . . .

Years later we became good friends, and we laughed about the "pedestal of perfume" I had once accused her of standing on. More surprisingly, I turned out to have a few shopping instincts of my own. I never became very knowledgeable about clothes in general, but I did have strong feelings about shirts. I actually preferred some to others. I was the first Canadian to like plaid shirts (well, one of the first), except for the ones I hated—the ones that "looked like pajamas." Later, under the tutelage of another prime shopper in LA, I came out of my shell and began to really relish a fine shirt. As fate would have it I turned out to have expensive taste, but my motley career path hardly ever gave me much money, so what I wore didn't reflect what I liked (something that may be true of more men than you think). Then another woman introduced me to thrift stores, and of course, I'm still with her. She also made me buy my first linen jacket ($5 at a giant Goodwill), and only when I wore it did I understand her description of that cool fabric. I'm pretty good in a thrift store now, but I still bow to her greater natural talent, as she cruises a long rack of men's shirts, while with a combination of her eye and her hand she somehow detects anything that is my size and nice.

I also came to another realization, I think it was in my twenties. It occurred to me that some of the things I enjoyed most about women were the direct result of shopping. I liked how they smelled, I liked how they looked in their clothing and how they looked as it came off, I took pleasure in the million ways they did their hair, their eyes, their lips. How could I be in favor of those things and pretend to be against shopping?

So finally I became a decent shopping companion. It's true I still favor outings that have a specific target, but I have improved, really I have. I've been known to patrol a hobby store, looking for a certain color of bugle bead, and find it for my tired lady; and I once dove into an acre of purse displays and came back with a slim black Fossil bag with the long shoulder strap she was dreaming of.

If I've tried to learn one thing, it's the subtle art of helping a shopper figure out which dress, or which knee brace, *she* really wants.

And that's why I'm here, talking to you from these pages. I think I can help you with this interesting challenge of shopping for a guy to love. I can help steer you through the vast herd of men to the right one. And I can help you overcome the factors that sometimes make shopping tougher than it needs to be.

Because even a good shopper can use a guide, when the thing you're seeking comes in a bewildering variety and has many ill-understood virtues and flaws, and when the shopping process is a bit more convoluted than usual. Not to mention that scams are in the air and must be resisted. There's a lot of misinformation out there on men and love, and your excursion is more likely to succeed if you have the real skinny on both.

In Part One, I examine the nature of the man-beast, separating the myths from the facts about testosterone, the male ego, and the surprising ways men open up about their feelings. Part Two then looks at shopping criteria: the *x* factor that is more important than status, why new isn't always improved, the unique advantages of shopping for someone who is shopping for you, and what it means to find a love you can afford. In Part Three, the shopping fun begins with a chapter called "Shop, and always shop." I then explore what your dream man hopes you will do to steer toward him, why you can and should often take the initiative in real-world encounters, and the unexpected value of having someone else proxy-shop for you. In Part Four, I present a simple, realistic way to choose the right dating site and find the guy for you on it, and describe five good sites. And I explain how to get around the number one problem posed by pay sites, the contact barrier.

Once you've met a good prospect, online or off, we arrive at the all-important and much-neglected trial period, described in Part Five. It's the first six months to a year, during which you do an amazing thing: you test love by trying love. I provide twelve intriguing activities that bring out a couple's true colors, along with tips for assessing the state of the union at regular intervals, including how to get the Carfax report on your new dude.

The trial period raises some burning questions, which I answer in Part Five:

- If you fall in love, does that prove you're with the right guy?

- Why do people sometimes rush the relationship, even when they've agreed not to? Does this indicate a deeper problem, and can it be solved?

- Why does a guy suddenly disappear when things were going so well? Is it commitment-phobia or something else?

- Should you judge a man by what he is now, or by what he could be?

- If you have fights, does that mean it's not going to work out?

I close the book with two chapters related to long-term satisfaction, the first on shopping addiction and how to overcome it, and the second on the best-kept secret of couples who last: how to opt out of the "perfect bliss" game that no one can win, and go for real love instead.

You know how to shop, how to make the fine distinctions and look in the right places. But maybe you haven't always approached mate finding that way. You sometimes leave it to chance, let it slip way too far down on your to-do list, or you get in a rush, throw out all your rational faculties and fall for the last guy you could really spend your life with. But we're going to change that. I'll be your coach, guide, and cheerleader to spark your shopping synapses for this particular quest. I'll help you focus on who you're really looking for and how to join hearts with him, in a way that will maximize your chances for a love that lasts.

So let's go shopping, you and I.

PART
ONE

THE NATURE OF THE MAN-BEAST

1

testosterone is your friend

Testosterone is the fizz in the man drink.

It's a kind of ancient moonshine, running through the blood of men and making them excitable.

But testosterone has fallen on hard times, and a woman shopping for a man may be confused as to whether it's good or bad. Or even there.

It's not easy to remember, as you watch a modern man walking from the parking lot to the office building across the street, with his iPhone and his pleasant clothes and his eyeglasses, that you're looking at a creature who rose from the caves and the jungles to conquer the planet. But you are. A brawny seeker who crossed the seas in stout ships, built the great railroads, the highways, the skyscrapers, invented the crossbow and the steel smelter, and fought savage wars over territory and plunder. It's hard to remember when he puts on his jammie pants of tartan plaid and shuffles around the house in the middle of the night that that tartan was worn by burly warriors who came over the hill dressed in kilts, terrifying the enemy with the sound of bagpipes.

And as you deal with the modern male in many of his shapes—computer geeks, bureaucrats, nurses, house-husbands—it's hard to imagine he has the same juices flowing through him that he had back then. But he does; those juices just aren't quite sure what to do with themselves these days. Though they do show themselves in the night when he sees your naked body and his face is flushed with desire and he mashes his lips upon you and you make frenzied love.

Testosterone helps make men different from women. You have it too, but we have more of it. That's why men are bigger, stronger, smellier, hairier, and harder to marry. That's right, extra testosterone in the womb causes men's ring fingers to be longer than women's, so the ring has farther down to go to be well and truly attached.[1] In both sexes, testosterone helps puberty transform us from angels to animals, and in adulthood it makes for health and energy, including a healthy libido.

But there's a dark twist to the story: testosterone is a peppery drug, redolent of bulls and matadors. It facilitates aggression and violence and contributes to reckless decision making. Most fascinatingly, as you may have observed, its levels are directly affected by life's ups and downs. When a man gets sexually aroused, his testosterone rises. When he wins in a competition it goes up; when he loses it goes down. When he gets into a fight it rises, and if he wins, it rises even more. *A guy feels good when his testosterone is high.* In fact, he feels high. Testosterone is nature's Viagra; it is nature's anabolic steroid—and I suspect that high testosterone levels are addictive. If you want to know what it feels like to be a guy with elevated testosterone, try downing fifteen cups of

---

1. Longer relative to the length of the index finger. Typically, those two fingers are about equal in length in women; men have the ring finger longer. All sorts of claims are being made these days about the significance of this finger ratio, from what toys babies prefer (balls versus dolls) to what a person's sexual orientation is. Google it and enjoy.

black coffee, put on an animal-skin vest and not much else, and run through the town with your brothers, beating on a djembe.

Sound good? You know it does. At least to men.

But the world is not so friendly to testosterone these days. Its stock has fallen. Success at school, at work, and in the family increasingly does not encourage wildness, feistiness, and impulsiveness. Most jobs don't need brawn, and even wars are fought in a more technological way, with much less hand-to-hand combat and much less loss of life. Less glory for the high-test male. Testosterone loves competition; it loves hierarchies where you know exactly who is your boss and who you are the boss of; it loves patriarchy. It doesn't do so well in environments where everyone is supposed to work together and everyone gets to express their opinion, and where a constant attempt to one-up other people—or prove you're "better" than them—is seen as being in bad taste. In other words, today's world.

But men still crave that addictive rush. That's why, I believe, testosterone has been driven into a sort of symbolic ghetto, where boys and men play violent video games and watch violent sports played by others, with the passion inverse to the participation. And we get sports' latest gift to science, Ultimate Fighting, a brave attempt to prove that the brain really is essential to higher thought by subjecting it to repeated pummeling ("striking") and oxygen deprivation ("submissions"). Ultimate Fighting is as raw and elemental as our suburban lifestyle is not: just two guys beating each other into bloody pulps while the crowd in the coliseum cheers. (Although its proponents claim it is safer than "the sweet science"—boxing—I think the jury is still out on how this new crop of pummeled brains will fare in a decade or two.) I watch it sometimes, I have my favorites (I like the underdog who pulls off the surprise submission), and it probably raises my testosterone levels.

On the upside, testosterone is brave and generous, it will die for its allies (and loved ones), and it can coalesce men into a magnificent team, but it prefers to have another team as the enemy, and it likes a clear chain of command like in the army.

So what is a shopper to think?

As a woman wondering what to look for in a man, testosterone is your friend—up to a point. You want your guy to lust after you. You want him to take out the garbage and stack those heavy boxes. You want him to bond with other men, within reason. You want him to defend you in the unlikely event that you are physically attacked. You want him to stand up for himself and not be a doormat, certainly not your doormat. But it would also be nice if he could hold a job, work and play well with others, and treat you as an equal.

So there's a balance one would want between too little and too much of the high-octane stuff. Here are some tips on how to achieve it in your choice of a man.

Don't pick a guy who doesn't seem like a man, in your eyes. That doesn't mean he has to be a big bad football player, a tough guy good with his fists, or a rampaging CEO who swallows lesser beings like a shark. But he has to seem manly to *you*. And here is a pointer about that. Most men have some area in which they won't back down. Something they'll go to the wall for. For one guy it might be his personal honor: if jostled by another man he will square off and raise his fists. For another guy it might be about how people treat each other—he just won't stand for cruelty. That's a good one. For another guy it may be words. Maybe he's into logic and he will fight to the death against a specious argument. For another it's serving his family and his friends. What matters is that you locate this backbone in him and that it is to your taste—so you will feel he has a bedrock of masculinity that you can count on, and just as important, he will feel affirmed by you. If the areas that enlist his manly hormones don't matter to you, he won't survive as a man in your eyes.

Testosterone can be triggered in the service of almost any challenge—even, perhaps, controlling testosterone. The ideal man has enough of a governor over it to avoid running amok. A great and historic example: in October 1962 America's arch-enemy, Russia, had installed deadly missiles on the island of Cuba, close enough to hit the U.S. east coast. President John F. Kennedy was faced with testosterone running rampant in a gang of trigger-happy generals and Pentagon types who were itching to react in ways everyone knew would likely lead to full-blown nuclear war. Against all odds, Kennedy had the strength to keep them under control, look at other options, and find a solution. We don't know if he achieved this because

1. He had less testosterone than the hawks.

2. He had more testosterone and channeled it into opposing them.

3. He had as much as them but had a governor on it, and that governor was a kind of rationality, a regard for the welfare of the many.[2]

I suspect that more and more men these days are learning to channel part of their testosterone into a control mechanism that reins in the rest. They're learning how to enlist their hormone in a battle against its own excesses.

---

2. The true story is told in the political thriller *Thirteen Days* (2000), one of the best meditations on testosterone ever to appear on film.

Not to be outdone in this regard, nature has built some clever checks and balances into the male, to better equip him for the normal course of love. If you understand them, you can avoid trouble. When a guy is first going after you, and is seized with lust or the desire for a conquest, his testosterone goes up and he may behave like a crazed peacock. Even when he falls in love, as long as you remain unattained, his edge is only increased. But if you give your heart to him, a strange thing happens. His testosterone goes down a tad. That accounts for the strange sensation a guy gets, of returning to a state of innocence, of not feeling as predatory in a sexual way. He becomes more tender, more romantic, more softened around the edges. He may get out his lute and sing you a pretty song. At that very moment nature makes your testosterone rise, so you are more like him. You two meet in the middle and you feel as if you are right for each other in a way that no one else in the world could be.

Speaking of being alike, take your own testosterone levels into account in choosing a man. There is no exact formula for this, but it could go one of two ways. If you have a lot of the stuff, you may want a guy who is also high-test. Because you don't want to have more than him. Or it could go the other way: I've seen couples where it's pretty apparent that the woman liked construction toys when she was a girl and the guy liked dolls, but darn it, they have amazing sexual polarity—they positively sizzle for each other. And yes, I noticed her ring finger was ginormous . . . I think this is the exception, though, and I think she found him scintillatingly manly in wonderful ways.

Back to nature's balancing act. When the initial flare of being in love subsides, hormones return to their normal levels. But a second adjustment takes place when marriage and kids come into the picture. Married men, especially fathers, have less testosterone coursing through them. And that's a good thing, because higher octane levels are associated with less time and energy devoted to a man's family.

With all this in mind, the wise woman will resolve not to look nature's gift horse in the mouth. She will vow to welcome the time when her man becomes more domestic, and won't put him down for not being such a bad boy anymore. But she will also resolve to nurture his testosterone, if "nurture" and "testosterone" can be used in the same sentence.

Some of the methods are already in place, some may not be. Support him so he doesn't undergo needless defeats—those are bad for his levels. Arouse him sexually so that he feels the sap running through him. Don't shame him for wanting to watch the occasional violent sport. Don't let him wear tight underpants. Don't become his boss if you can avoid it. Above all, celebrate the moments when he fights for the principles that you originally loved in him. Or when he overcomes fear and risks it all. Oh, and keep him away from food or drink in clear plastic containers made with BPA, especially heated in the microwave![3]

All this presumes a likeable dude with his hormones in a good place. But you also have to look out for the opposite. And that would be a guy with high testosterone levels who doesn't have a suitable outlet for them. Watch for this character and steer clear of him. He's spoiling for the contest that will allow him to prove himself, but the contest isn't forthcoming. So he may take it out on you, by trying to turn you into the enemy he vanquishes, or he may get so involved in the NFL that he has no time for a relationship. Another example: high testosterone is associated with the performer—the person who

---

3. Bisphenol A, found in hard clear plastic containers, can leach into the blood and block testosterone.

craves a huge audience and a lot of attention—and a man who never got that going may expect you to supply it, by being his adoring spectator.

And then there's licorice. When you find a good man and you like the testosterone running through him, if he occasionally goes over the top, just slap some licorice into his mouth. It contains glycyrrhizinic acid, which has been proven to take the edge off. This is even truer for women, so when you want to make him feel especially manly, you may want to chew some licorice yourself.

2

the male ego

how to shop for the one that suits you

$\mathcal{D}$o you want your male ego in a large, a medium, or a small?

This is one of those situations where size matters. Where it pays to ask a Goldilocks type of question: "Is it too small to suit me, or too big to suit me, or is it just right?"[1]

Maybe you've used this approach before, when faced with another male appendage, or even when appraising the whole smiling hunk of beef that stands before you, seeking your company.

In either case, different women are going to reach different verdicts depending on their own dimensions and needs. And that's the way it should be. This kind of test is tailored to you.

And here's another male part it works on.

A male ego can be large, medium, or small. Or extra-large. That's a fun one.

Before you decide which size you want, we should take a look at how they perform in practical terms—the problems and advantages of each.

---

1. The pattern is found in many versions of "Goldilocks and the Three Bears" and other fairy tales, where one choice is too *x*, another is not *x* enough, and the third is just right.

THE MEDIUM EGO

Let's take medium first. It's the innocuous choice, the one least likely to stir up trouble. A guy with a medium-sized ego has a pretty good opinion of himself, but he knows his own limitations too. He doesn't feel superior to other humans. And the issue of "who is better" isn't always on his mind. He's fully capable of admiring others and giving them credit. He's a good listener. He is not always caught up in competition.

He sounds dreamy, doesn't he? Is there any *problem* with this guy?

Well, that depends on you. You may, for example, find him lacking in ambition, which is often driven by a desire to live up to one's high opinion of oneself. If you are a go-getting woman and want a mate who is like you, you may not be satisfied with a man whose talents find no spur in his relaxed self-rating. Or you may *not* be ambitious, but you may for that exact reason crave a guy who is, a partner whose restless energy complements your more mellow nature.

Bear this in mind: **A man who wears a medium ego is more likely to be able to get caught up in things that are not about himself.** Like places you might want to explore, like what happened to you today, like vacations, like your sexual needs.

But on the other hand, he ain't gonna bring you the world and lay it at your feet.

THE LARGE EGO

Which calls up our next candidate, the man with the big ego. What's he got to offer? Will you end up toasting him with champagne or trying to find the exit?

That depends on what comes *with* that mighty self-image.

Like merit. We don't mind a big ego in a guy who finds a cure for pneumonia. Or has a vision of racial equality that changes the world. "I have a dream," Dr. King said, which could sound self-important. Why should the rest of us, the hundreds of thousands gathered on the National Mall and as part of the watching world, care about his dream? Well, because he had the confidence to make us care about it. (And oh yes, he had a good dream. That matters too.)

To take on the mantle of leadership, to want to be the one who makes the hard decisions that everyone else will follow, requires a rather high opinion of oneself. You have to think you're the best one for the job, or as they say in sports, you have to *want the ball.*

Otherwise you'll be so stressed out by your position of command, so busy trying to pass the buck, that you'll develop an ulcer or allow bad choices to be made.

So what does that have to do with choosing a guy? Well, **before you reject a man for having a big ego, take note of what he is actually accomplishing every day.** Is he managing a team well, charting a smart course that leads to good results? More power to him. As I mentioned before, do you want a man of ambition and achievement, either because you are that same breed or because you aren't? Then a guy with a big ego may be a good catch for you.

What about other kinds of merit? They count too. Find someone who is really, really good at anything difficult—be it playing the cello, brain surgery, or professional tennis—and you'll probably find a person who thinks pretty well of himself. (Or herself—we'll get to the female ego in a moment.)

So far so good. A large ego with merit to match can be a good thing. But is it always?

Not when a man gets a "swelled head" and starts to focus more on his own godlike stature than on the job he is supposed to be doing. That can make him reckless. We don't lack for famous examples in recent history: the names Tiger Woods and John Edwards and Bill Clinton come to mind. Men who couldn't resist the siren call to their egos, even if it would harm their wives and families, damage the careers they had fought hard to build, or even, as in Clinton's case, alter the fate of the Western world.[2]

A fatal slip sometimes occurs in the male psyche. It's the slip from "I am proud because I'm trying my very best and doing a good job" to "I am proud because my performance proves that I am a god who can do no wrong, and others had better bow down when they see me or I'll fire their sorry asses." That is a perilous shift in direction. Instead of focusing on the job and on honest effort, one focuses on oneself and one's greatness.

Self-confidence shades into arrogance.

That ain't gonna cut it.

Which brings up a crucial giveaway. To detect whether the big shot you're dating has the goods, notice *how he treats his underlings.* (And if you can't observe him on the job, how he talks about them.) A good leader gives thanks every day for the people who work under him. He appreciates their hard work; he celebrates their talents and comes up with amazing ways those talents can be used. He doesn't resent their most brilliant exploits, isn't threatened by them. And he shares information with them, so his lieutenants can make the right decision when he isn't there. Oh, and when it's time to give out credit, he happily spreads it around—because he really believes that it is due.

---

2. Without the Lewinsky scandal it is very possible that we never would have had the eight-year presidency of one George W. Bush, the effects of which—whatever you think of them—may never be undone.

But beware the man who

- disparages his helpers

- picks on their little mistakes, even when they are doing their best and producing good work

- is stingy with thanks and credit

- tells them what to do but doesn't explain why, because he doesn't think they need to know (they do)

THE EXTRA-LARGE EGO

You run into the extra-large ego when a large ego is not accompanied by real merit: when a man's actual worth falls way short of his self-image. He isn't very good at what he does; he's a chronic underachiever who for some reason has developed an exalted picture of himself and needs to maintain it at any cost.

This guy is not a barrel of laughs. Fortunately, he isn't hard to recognize. The key is that *he needs to compensate for his mediocrity by putting up some kind of smoke screen.* Here are some methods I've noticed:

- He can't stop talking about how great he is.

- He has to keep telling the same story about how so-and-so shafted him when it mattered most (this can be twenty years ago).

- He takes great pleasure in despising groups he thinks are lesser than himself.

- He reports the exploits of other people (usually famous) as if they were his own.

This last one is fascinating. Maybe it's a football team, or a football star. Our hollow man recites what the quarterback did today, how he made that impossible pass, and you sense an overzealous quality in his voice, a mad timbre, and you realize he is counting every victory as proof of his own worth. His words are "Look what he did out there on the field today," but his meaning is "Look what I did out there." Being a fan is one thing, but this shades into crazier territory.

THE SMALL EGO

That leaves the small ego. We can deal with it quickly, because it is so rare!

It's sometimes called humility. It is a decorous lack of pride, and in moderation it is admirable.

When it goes too far, it becomes lack of self-confidence, diffidence, even cowardice. A desire to flagellate oneself, maybe a guilt complex. Not so good.

Or it becomes its opposite. An ego starved for attention and praise, a tiny thing raging in the night, wanting revenge on the world. But that is the same as our extra-large.

THE FEMALE EGO

Now, what about the female ego? Do these sizes apply to it as well? I'm sorry to say they do, though maybe not always so blatantly. Okay, I'm not sorry. But yes, most of what I've said so far applies equally to women.[3] So it behooves the canny shopper to ask herself some hard questions about what size she wears, and what size in a man may fit her best.

That may still leave you thinking, "J.M., you've left something out. There's something else about the male ego that *isn't* equally true of women—something important."

You're right, and I'll cover it next. It will lead us into a very interesting area, male vulnerability and whether males can be open about it. We'll uncover some surprises there.

THE MALE EGO AT ITS MALE-EST: AGGRESSION AND VULNERABILITY

"Everything was going fine, and then his male ego got in the way." I've often heard women say this. What do they mean?

First, they may mean what a plain-talking female friend of mine calls "dick stretching." This tendency really irks her. She means a man being competitive when it isn't necessary or helpful, especially in the presence of another man who is gratuitously seen as some kind of threat. A social gathering can be going nicely, everybody's having a good time, and then two men start bashing their antlers together like rutting stags in a spring meadow. Or maybe a man has great job opportunities but he always ends up in conflict with a boss or co-worker. Or he's in a relationship with you and you find that you are reduced to a supporting role, because he always has to be the lead.

There's a lot of this going around, but not all men are prone to it—not even most men. And the good news is, when you're getting

---

3. One point that doesn't so much: the tendency to celebrate one's own godlike status by reckless behavior, particularly by having affairs. Those forms of acting out may be attributable to our old friend testosterone.

to know a guy, you can detect whether this kind of thing is likely to become a problem, based on the ego sizing that we discussed before. Look for that man who wears an extra-large, the one whose inflated self-image seems oddly out of whack with his lack of objective achievement. He's a good bet for the dick-stretching Olympics, and you may want to scratch him off your list.

Men and vulnerability

The second way the male ego can get its owner in trouble is more subtle and more poignant, thankfully. It's also easier to deal with, as I'll explain, and therefore doesn't have to be a deal-breaker.

It is this: we men often have difficulty confessing our own vulnerability, and in an effort to hide it, we resort to behaviors that we don't really mean, which only make things worse.

Here are two examples of situations where this can arise:

A. A man is struggling with a challenge and losing; he sees failure bearing down on him.

B. A man is laid low by something someone has said or done.

Boys are trained (mostly by other boys) not to show weakness. The awful emotions that are linked with failure—fear, shame, sadness—are just the ones they aren't supposed to show. Same with having their feelings hurt, especially "by a girl." The other guys would laugh at that. *And the other guys are never really gone.* You will understand men better if you imagine that they live life with a sort of phantom gang of boys lurking on the sidelines, ready to cheer or heckle.

They enforce a thing I'll call the boy code. The boy code absolutely and emphatically insists on two things:

- Never be like a girl.

- Never have tender feelings for another boy.

(In case you're wondering, it also urges a boy to always be brave, strong, good at sports, and loyal, and in some versions, to never grow up.)

When a man takes a punch from life, it would be better from these boys' point of view if he could react with anger. That's a very acceptable emotion to them. But sometimes he tries that and can't make it stick. Honesty forces him to own the problem. Or he's just too badly wounded to get mad.

Let's break down the way the male ego presents in these situations: how your man will act, what he really needs, and what you can offer him.

In scenario A, life has thrown him a curve he doesn't think he can handle; maybe an important project he's been working on has taken a bad turn and he can't see a way through. Maybe he just heard that layoffs are coming and he's going to be one of them. For whatever reason, he's reeling with a sense that he may fail. In scenario B, he has suffered a slight of some kind, and it stung. The two can go together: failure itself, no matter how private it is (even if it's just you staring into a computer screen at a software that refuses to do what you desperately need it to do), can feel like humiliation.

Okay, so this has happened to your man and he's deep in some combination of hurt, shame, sadness, and maybe fear that directly involves his ego.

And you walk into the room at six p.m. and he's there. He is silent, not doing much, and at first you don't notice that anything is wrong, especially if you are in the middle of changing your clothes, talking on your cell phone, or checking your email. But after a while you notice he isn't responding in a normal way to stimuli. Is he acting numb or acting surly? You're not sure.

So you say, "Are you okay?"

And he says, "Yeah." After a pause he mumbles, "Not really."

"Do you want to talk about it?"

"Not really."

He's speaking with half a personality, like someone just gave him a chemical that will shortly paralyze him.

What you're seeing is actually the male ego at its most primal, a boyish defense mechanism in an adult male. *He's trying not to cry.* If he opens up about this, he may cry. If he cries, the phantom boys will annihilate him.

Several things can happen at this point. Maybe you kindly leave him alone, realizing where he's at. That would be cool. Or you try to be kind by pressing him to talk. That won't go well. Or you interpret his behavior as hostile and you react with anger. Maybe words are exchanged.

But what happened was he got hurt. And he tried to hide the fact that he could get hurt—that he was that vulnerable—by not showing *any* feelings. How can he open up when the intense emotions he is in the grip of are forbidden by the boys' tribunal?

And you're right: he may need help, or consolation, or reassurance, or a listening ear. He just doesn't want them *yet*. Here's what he wants to do: he wants to recover from the emotional tailspin he's in, begin to feel like himself again, and start to see light ahead. Accept the setback, and maybe even start to see a solution. And at that precise moment, when the sky is clearing, he may seek you out and want to tell you what a hairy precipice he survived. And that's just when you may not realize that what he's doing is *talking about his feelings,* in the form of a story.

Men will tell you how scared they were, how much pain they were in, how ashamed they felt; they just aren't likely to tell you while it's happening. But it makes a great story once they can give it a positive spin and say they've gotten past it, absorbed the blow, figured a way forward. It's a tale of adventure and survival; it's cool.

And I'm not even talking about all men here. Some men *can* talk about these kinds of feelings even while they're in the throes of them. Maybe that's because, like some women, they didn't pass through the gender-tilted gauntlets of youth as easily as most, and so began to loose those bonds.

Meanwhile I can hear a chorus of pundits saying, WAIT JUST A MINUTE HERE, YOU CAN'T SLIP THIS BY US. MEN TALKING ABOUT THEIR FEELINGS? GET *OUT* OF HERE!

So I'll face the issue head on, in the next chapter.

3

but really now, do men talk about their feelings?

*W*e read all the time that men don't talk about their feelings. Many of the self-help books say this. The top seller as I write this, *Act Like a Lady, Think Like a Man,* says it right on page 50. Men don't vent. Sitcoms and comedians bray their agreement (because so much comic hay can be made out of the supposed gulf between men and women). But you know what? It's horse poop.

Men do talk about their feelings.

A fine example of this happened on *60 Minutes*—maybe you saw it too. About a month after the Deepwater Horizon oil rig exploded on April 20, 2010, in the Gulf of Mexico, one of the last men to escape the rig alive, Mike Williams, was interviewed. Williams was the chief electronics technician on the rig. In the interview he talks about mistakes that were made leading up to the explosion, but what interests me here is his riveting account of his own showdown with death on the terrible night. He's a likeable, salt-of-the-earth kind of guy, a manly sort, with an open face and a reddish goatee. As he tells the story, he doesn't just convey what happened, he relives it in astonishing detail and with every emotion plain on his face. At several moments, hit by fiery explosions and pinned by a door, he "knows" he is going to die, and he expresses the horror of this with utter candor. Then he reaches a decision point where he must stay on the rig or jump into the ocean a hundred feet below. As he tells of his terror and his love for his family, and the moment when he prayed that his wife and little girl would know he tried everything he could to survive—tears roll down his cheeks. And then he jumps into the oily sea. If there was ever a better example of open, honest emotion, I haven't seen it.[1]

So yes, in their own way and at their own time, men even talk about the most personal and painful feelings.

But that's just the tip of the iceberg.

Because most human conversation is about feelings. I'm a little sick today, I've got this ache in my back, I just saw the most amazing catch in the ninth inning, that stupid painter screwed up the railing, those liberals are at it again, I met the most amazing woman last night, those conservatives are at it again, my supervisor is a meatball . . . and so on.

I've known a lot of men and I've had a lot of conversations with them, and I have to say a whole lot of it was venting. Guys have bent my ear with raw emotion on every conceivable topic, venting anger and joy, grief and relief, worry and yes, more worry. I've sat in a guy's basement apartment while he told me about his parents' relationship and he got really sad and cried a bit. Guys love to share their hopes too, partly because that is a good way to stoke them up and build a feeling of optimism. I had a friend, we would get together for Mexican food every now and then, and after I finished complaining about my problems, he would tell me how his home business was

---

1. Visit http://www.cbsnews.com/stories to watch the interview.

finally picking up steam, more clients were signing up, he was on the verge of upgrading his hardware (and we'd go into the technicalities of that), and the whole dialog was like a slow crescendo, an effort to buck up his own spirits and feel more hopeful about the future. It was pure emotion, and we both knew what it was for, and it paid off because it's easier to try hard when you have optimism.

Why have I been the recipient of so much male emoting? Let's see: I'm unthreatening, a pretty good listener, able to understand what is being shared with me, curious about the things that interest my friends, and unlikely to condemn them for what they're feeling. And I'm not a threat to hug them when they're hurting. Not so hard, huh?

Let me expand on a few of these factors.

A good listener

You're more likely to be a good listener if you *want* your guy to share his emotions with you. But maybe you don't. Some women don't. They subscribe to that same guy code that boys enforce; they are more comfortable with a "man of action" who is befuddled by emotions, because that strikes them as manly and darn it, it turns them on.[2] They like the strong silent type, whose only betrayal of emotion when his beloved beagle has to be put to sleep is a slight quiver of the lip. That's cool, but they're going to have to imagine a lot of his biography, because he won't be telling it to them.

As for the rest of you, who would like it if your man would share with you the things that move him to joy or anger, here are a couple of suggestions.

---

2. The guy code is what's left of the boy code when it has been tempered by romance and other plot twists of adulthood.

Be aware, take notice, when he gets to the place where he wants to talk about something close to the bone. Keep in mind, as I said earlier, that he may have to right himself before he can tell you how his emotional boat capsized. When he does approach you with what seems to be a lighthearted story that features some setback (especially a story that expresses intense relief), watch out for the possibility that he is spilling his guts. Stay with him, let him tell it his way.

Stay with him. If you can, give him the time he has forgotten to ask for, just as you might forget if you busted in on him with some emotional crisis.

Finally, keep in mind that the things he feels strongly about may sometimes not be your biggest areas of fascination. Men and women have a lot more overlap in their interests than they're given credit for, and well-matched couples have a whole merry boatload of overlap, but still, some of his rant-worthy topics won't be at the top of your list of things you were hoping to hear about today. But if you make the effort to borrow his passion and empathize, the dividends will be huge when he has something on his mind that you do desperately want to hear about.

(This advice can of course be reversed, with no caveats. Read it to him if he doesn't return the listening favor.)

Unlikely to condemn him for what he's feeling

There's a huge one. A guy won't spill his guts to you if he thinks you're too easy to offend or you're going to pass judgment on him. This may not be your fault: for example, he may be afraid he'll look like a sissy in your eyes if he betrays any vulnerability, when you in fact don't hold men to that ridiculous standard. Make sure he knows that, in no uncertain terms.

Nevertheless, many of us do judge our partners harshly, and we're so busy interrupting with comments like "That was a dumb thing to do" or "Great, now you've made her think badly of me too" that it's no wonder we never get to hear the whole story, and our partner is just that much less likely to risk total honesty with us the next time.

Not trying to hug him

Don't offer motherly sympathy to a guy who thinks he has an objective problem. You may want to put your arms around him and say "There, there," but this implies that the problem is how he's *feeling*. He doesn't think so. He thinks the problem is the thing that happened at work, or what his computer won't do, or what so-and-so said about him that rang horribly true and made everyone snicker. So if you take him to your bosom, you're striking the wrong note; he may feel as if you are belittling his plight. Like he's a little boy who scuffed his knee and thinks he's mortally wounded.

Motherly sympathy can also be counterproductive if the guy is desperately trying to keep a rein on his emotions, because it may put him over the edge. On the other hand, if a man ever looks at you with tears in his eyes, if he is in that rare state of grace where a guy is ready and willing to cry about something he feels deeply, whether it's the death of his dad or the birth of his daughter, go ahead and hug him . . .

Strike that. It still may not be the right thing to do. Let me explain.

I can't tell you how many times in my life I have wanted to cry and I couldn't. Or how I've envied my spouse her ability to let the tears flow when she is discouraged or feels ill done by or is moved by the plight of another living creature, human or otherwise. She gets catharsis, she gets release, she gets washed clean. So many times I carry grief or despair around in me like a big aching lump and I can't get rid of it. But when I have those lucky times that I feel something with the right keening edge and I cry, and she is right there in front of me, I am still better off if she just watches with understanding, not panicking and not rushing to comfort me. I am usually talking at the same time, and my words are doing the trick just fine; my tears don't need any more help.

Maybe your guy is different. Maybe he never cries, or maybe when he does, he wants an arm around him. You'll figure it out.

A man is basically a cauldron of emotions. Lift the lid and enjoy!

4

yeah, but men don't like to talk about *relationships*, right?

Saying men don't like to talk about relationships is another of those clichés that do nothing but confuse the sexes about how to deal with each other.

But I've heard people defend it, in several ways.

First they argue that men can't *understand* relationships. And I'll admit, that would certainly be a setback on the road to talking about them—if it were true.

Fortunately it's a ridiculous claim. To begin with, what about all the men who have been psychologists, psychiatrists, therapists, and counselors—from Dr. Freud to Dr. Phil? Do we really want to claim that this small army has no insight into relationships?

Then there are the male writers, down through the ages, of plays and novels and that fine modern art form, the screenplay. In his play *Hamlet,* Shakespeare is said by some critics to have invented the modern psyche, and his emotional insights still amaze.

Closer to home, I think of movies like *Kissing a Fool* and *My Best Friend's Wedding. Kissing a Fool* (1998) tells the story of two men who are best friends, sportscaster Max and novelist Jay. Max falls in love with Jay's gorgeous female editor, Samantha, and though it is Jay who we eventually realize belongs with Samantha, Jay tries to support his friend. Starring David Schwimmer, Jason Lee, Mili Avital, and the irreplaceable Bonnie Hunt, it's a hilarious, slap-happy guy comedy, and it's one of the wisest studies ever put on screen of what makes two people compatible. Who wrote it? James Frey, the guy who got in so much trouble with Oprah when he was caught mixing fiction into a memoir. But that doesn't diminish the brilliance of his relationship movie.

Then there is *My Best Friend's Wedding* (1997). This was a major hit, for good reason. As you probably know, it's a cynical, suave tale about a woman (Julia Roberts) who sets out to sabotage the wedding of her best friend (Dermot Mulroney), whom she belatedly decides she loves. Really it's a dazzling investigation of the eternal gap between friendship and romantic love. It mostly (and very effectively) takes the Julia Roberts character's point of view, and it was written by a man. Ron Bass is his name, the same guy who co-wrote *Rain Man*, one of the greatest movies ever about *male* emotions.

I can hear someone responding, "Well, writers are different from ordinary people. They feel things more deeply." (I actually heard this said by a songwriter in Nashville—you know who you are.) But it isn't true. Writers have the same feelings as everybody else: they just have a creative streak (and usually a deep love of others' writing), which makes them put those feelings into art. If non-writers didn't have the same feelings, why would millions of regular people gobble up the best works of every age—like the movies I just mentioned?

What about ordinary men who trudge the earth and toil for their daily bread? Do they understand, or care about, relationships? Um, yes. Men, like women, are very curious about how others get along—whether as friends, couples, family members, or coworkers, and they like to observe the tangled interactions and try to guess what is happening and explain it. We are all gossips or at least "interested spectators," and as armchair psychologists we sharpen our tools on our friends. It would be strange if men did not do this, because the ability to predict human behavior is a crucial survival skill, and understanding relationships is at the core of it.

Which brings up another point: men are also very astute about their *children's* relationships. My father didn't think of himself as an analytical guy, maybe because he was at home in the guy code, but every now and then he would settle a fight between his kids, or make a prediction about one of their friends, in a way that would cut right through all the posturing to the truth. I remember one night when my parents were out at a party, me and my fourteen-year-old sister—yes, that same older sister who first showed me the ways of shopping—got into a fairly savage conflict about what we would watch on TV, and at one point she tackled me and did a little damage to my admittedly scruffy shirt. Okay, I kept grabbing the remote and switching away from the old movie she was into that featured Bogart and Bergman, back to the cop show I wanted to watch. Okay, it was *Casablanca* and I was too dumb at twelve to like it. When my parents got home to some very upset kids, I was able to make the case that I was the injured one as my sister (and her attire) was unscathed. But that didn't pass muster with my father, who took me aside and said words to the effect of, "You are very good at pressing your sister's buttons and you need to rein that in, because she is vulnerable to it." I knew in an instant that he was right, and I took it to heart. How did he know so much about the dynamic between us, which I hardly thought he'd had a chance to observe? He wasn't a psychologist (he scoffed at that science) and he wasn't a writer. All he brought to the table was the acuity of a man who loved his children.

That leaves one more gambit for my imaginary debater. "Okay, men understand relationships, and they are interested in them. But a guy doesn't want to talk about his *own* relationship with his woman, right?"

Okay, you finally got me . . . the sitcoms are right. Guys just wander around thinking about sports and food and never even notice if their relationship is going badly. In my own life, I never notice if my spouse is cold or distant—I'm not aware of that at all. So of course I don't ask about it.

And cats can't hear a mouse in the next room.

Can we please stop repeating this stuff? The truth is, men and women are sensitive to the most minor changes in each other's emotional temperatures. Even over the phone, even over a cell phone, we can sense something amiss in our partner's tone of voice. We know what their normal, dealing-with-the-day, doing-fine voice sounds like, and if we hear something different, some lack of affect, our antennae twitch. And often our first thought is, "Did I screw up?" So we ask if anything's wrong, and we're actually relieved to find out that it's ordinary adversity—not us—that our beloved is contending with, and that they want to tell us about it.

But sometimes they sound evasive or frosty, and so we ask the dumbest-sounding, most popular question of all, "Are you mad at me?"

Do men ask this question? Of course we do, or it wouldn't be such a cliché. *Why* do we ask such a dangerous question? Because men, like other humans, treasure our closeness with our partners, and we don't want to lose it. So we wade into a conversation that we know may not be easy or safe, and may expose some bad behavior on our part, or may at least reveal that we've unintentionally hurt our partner's feelings. This kind of conversation can clear the air and can leave two people closer than ever, but it usually isn't much fun getting there.

The thing is, the alternative is even worse—to let the problem fester, to let a temporary wall start to become permanent.

But let's be clear, women are just as reluctant as men to get into dialogs where

1. They'll be hauled up in court and accused of being a bad person.

2. They'll be railroaded. If you think you won't get a fair hearing from your guy—that he won't listen to your side of the story—you are going to be reluctant. So is a man. Why would anyone want to listen to complaints if they won't get a chance to defend themselves?

3. The other person just wants to win. Unfortunately, some people bring out the gladiator in each other, the desire to fight to the death and never lose face, the truth be damned.

The good news is, many times when couples get in trouble, it's not because of malice or lack of love on either side, it's because of communication glitches—things one person is thinking, assuming, or doing that don't read the same to the other and have unintended effects. These unconscious slights can develop into thorny problems, but they can also be childishly easy to solve, if only they're brought into the light. If you were a man, which would you want: to have the problem escalate, or to hear what it is and be able to work it out? It's a no-brainer. Most guys, if they sense that things have slipped off-track with the woman they love, and there's any hope of setting things right by talking them over, are going to want to do that.

Experience helps here. Men (and women) who have ever been in a failed couple know that the time to talk about relationships is while there is still goodwill on both sides, and not too much bitterness to make open dialog possible. It's never pleasant or comfortable to have it out with your partner, but it's better than shutting down on each other. Men know this too, and if approached in good faith, will respond.

I'll talk more about this later, when we get to the topic of getting to know a prospective partner. It will turn out that a tiff or two is not such a bad thing—because it reveals so much about your potential as a couple.

5

are men aliens from Mars?

*W*hen you're young, in a glinting bar with your girlfriends and checking out the action, it's fun to think of guys as aliens. Dangerous, dazzling bad boys who are trying to put one over on you while you try to beat them at their own game. A lot of giggling and gasping and groaning happens on both sides, and both genders dress and act in a way that accentuates their differences. This dance of sex, this force field of seduction and evasion, gets its electric charge from the sense of a total gap separating males from females.

And our culture reinforces that idea: everything from dating lit to sitcoms keeps hammering home the message that men and women are two different species, they come from different planets, they speak different languages, they forever misunderstand each other— and isn't it hilarious that they do?

So this way of thinking gets entrenched. And when you're ready to find a life partner, you may conceive of him this way.

But here's the snag: **If you shop for an alien, you are liable to end up living with an alien.**

If you buy the premise, you're likely to accept a mate who is totally different from you, thinking there's no other way.

But couples end up being everyday partners, working together to build a life and often to raise children. And if you look at the happiest and most successful couples, do they look like aliens? Watch them as they sit in a restaurant. Watch them lean in close and talk, watch them laugh and grimace sympathetically, watch how they listen and how they are entertained. You can tell how well they know each other, how much they've been through and how much they will yet go through. They are pals, allies; they enjoy each other's company, they rely on each other. And when they're ordering food or eating it, it's almost comical how they complete each other's moves, unconscious of the fact that they can't help functioning as a team. They also have a physical closeness, they like to touch.

Contrast them with those two across the restaurant, who have trouble deciding where to sit, seem like two separate people when ordering, and have nothing to say during the meal. They hardly look at each other because it's embarrassing to not be talking. You're looking at two people who bought into the notion that men and women are aliens. They reveled in the fact that they had so little in common, believing that's how it was meant to be.

So it's a mistake to think of the male gender as some vast monolithic entity that is foreign to you. In these early chapters we've opened the owner's manual on men and taken a look around. So what's the verdict? Sure, men are different from women in many ways, but when you really look at them, aren't the differences *within* their ranks just as striking? We've seen that individual men have varying amounts of testosterone, and their fighting passion is invested in different things. The male ego comes in a variety of sizes and must be judged partly in relation to merit, which also varies wildly. Some men are better at communicating feelings and analyzing relation-ships than others (though men in general are not the slouches in this department that they're made out to be). Oddly enough, you could say most of these things about women too. Testosterone levels, ego sizes, communication skills—all vary among women. So certain women are going to match up better with certain men.

In fact, if you look at *adult* men and women, they don't seem as different from each other as boys and girls do. How can they, when they have to perform so many of the same roles? Speaking of that, when women are in professions that were thought to call for testos-terone, they seem to do awfully well. When you see a female litigator in court trouncing her male opponent, showing no mercy, no fear, no vulnerability, you have to wonder if maybe women don't need as much testosterone as men to be just as tough as men. It's almost as if they have a lower testosterone "threshold," to go with their lower testosterone.

Let's face it, when you're in a profession where showing weak-ness is counter-productive (say doctor, litigator, soldier, police officer, crisis manager, leader), you learn not to show weakness. If that wasn't already ingrained in you. That means lots of women seem to do pretty well with the boy code, in the right circumstances. Except that the terminology needs to be changed. The old boy code has to be re-expressed in gender-neutral terms: instead of "never act like a girl," it's "don't act weak, scared, vulnerable . . . at the wrong time." It's not always easy to say what the psychological differences are between men and women. Many characteristics once held to be biological—men are more rational, women are more emotional—have bitten the dust. The more society has opened up "male" avenues to women, the more we've discovered that what was thought to spring from nature actually yields to nurture.

At least we have the anatomical differences to fall back on—those are not going away, right? Maybe that's why society is a little desperate these days to assert them, and thus preserve *la difference*. Women have to work extra hard to go *beyond* nature, shaving, adorning, and displaying themselves so that men, with the help of Viagra and Cialis, can feel as if they are still aliens. I think society should chill a little. Men and women really are different in exquisite ways, some physical and some emotional, and each sex gets a kind of relief from interaction with the other. I think we can sleep at night knowing the distinctive savor each sex finds in the other is going to stick around. Nature put it there for a reason, and when a man and a woman fall in love, it fuels the feeling that this person is deliciously, achingly not you, yet at the same time you know their soul, you own it and they own yours.

News flash: men *and* women are from Venus, where sex is sexy and talk goes on all night.

Speaking of language, instead of thinking of it as a barrier between the sexes, we should celebrate it as the magnificent gift that it is, a gift that binds them together. After all, it isn't as if one of the sexes was left out of the verbal, brought along just as a beast of burden, unable to contribute to the conversation, like oxen. No, there's this beautiful shared talent. Some people have tried to claim that women have a greater linguistic facility than men, but that just shows how far astray social science can sometimes wander. Articulateness doesn't belong exclusively to either gender; it's something shared between them, one of the great miracles of the human species. There may be things women are more likely to express, and things men are, but that doesn't mean the other gender can't understand them or even revel in them.[1]

---

1. And our visit with male screenwriters might make the whole premise seem suspect.

I know a lawyer who loves hockey, is good at math, is high energy, reads a lot of science fiction, is a little kinky in bed, bakes really good bread, is tone-deaf, loves Jon Stewart, and has an awful fear of heights. Can you tell whether it's a man or woman? Both genders come in a million different types, and your job as a shopper is to find a guy who is *your* type.

A lot of dating lit for women, both books and magazines, tries to teach you the sneaky, clever techniques that supposedly work on all men. You're supposed to manipulate a guy to keep him interested, and lure him into your corral. But you wouldn't have to resort to all this artificial trickery if you had chosen the right guy. There are way too many guides on how to squeeze a square peg into a round hole.

I saw an article in a women's magazine that explained how to do subtle things in a bar to "attract a man," little adjustments in neckline and posture that "guys" can't resist. But the irony is, if you could get really good at attracting men in general—*all* men—that would just make it harder for you to find the right guy. If you draw all types of fish to your boat, that just makes it more difficult to catch the smallmouth bass you really want.

You already have something special that will attract your dream man if he gets a chance to experience you—something that won't register the same way to other men. Namely that you are you, and he is he. Given access to you, he will appreciate your soul and body—all of you—in a way that isn't attainable by most men. And it will happen as naturally as breathing. You won't need to use special tricks to trap him. Because being with you will set him free, and he will be at home with you in a way that most other men couldn't be.

The sexes are different, in delectable ways we all instinctively understand, and in mysterious ways we may never fully fathom. But far from being aliens, a man and a woman together are one of the most invincible forces on the planet.

Okay, we've opened the owner's manual on men and found that the stereotypes certainly don't do them justice. And I'm sure you're eager to get on with the actual shopping, to plunge into the marketplace and start selecting fabulous candidates for Life with You. But before we go there, I want to talk about *how* you're going to do the selecting. What shopping criteria are the best? And which ones don't work so well? That is Part Two.

PART
TWO

SHOPPING CRITERIA

6
shopping for status

*W*hether you're shopping for clothes or for a man, there is a certain temptation to key on what the world will think of your purchase rather than what you really think of it. Let's call it *shopping for status*. So you end up buying some bizarre dress that is very much in fashion, and your friends say it's fabulous, but in the end it doesn't make you happy, either because it doesn't really fit your figure and your coloring, or because it isn't really to your taste—you simply don't like it. This means you have a personal disagreement with Paris, or New York, or wherever it is that some committee has determined what shall be the rage this month.

And I say good for you. It was probably on some rainy Thursday in my youth that it dawned on me that every fall and every spring, my sister had to internalize the new rules of what was "in style" and what wasn't. This was the high-school version of fashion, not a world-class arena, but its rules were if anything more stringent, and they were enforced in a hormone-filled goldfish bowl where she lived in fear of the put-downs she would endure if she made the wrong choice. I know, because every night when we were cleaning the kitchen she would tell me of her plight, and ask me whether I liked her latest outfit or hairstyle, and complain about her friend Rhonda, who always seemed to have the right clothes (and an unlimited budget). I was appalled by how much effort and stress it cost her to try to conform to these standards—even what she went through every night with curlers in her beautiful straight hair was alarming to me.

But mostly I was perplexed. Because I thought beauty was eternal. Being a philosopher even at age fourteen, I thought that if a dress or a pair of jeans or a haircut was beautiful yesterday, then it's still beautiful today. The standards can't change every time the season turns. The Mona Lisa doesn't go from being a masterpiece to being second-rate because fall is coming.

The proof that I was right and the Paris Mafia are wrong is very simple: the fashionistas love to mock and scorn the styles of yesterday, but those are the very same styles they once pushed on the world. Everyone agrees now that certain eras of modern history were farcical. Even the customers. The seventies, with their flared pants and shag haircuts and platform shoes, are guffawed at by the same people who toed the line back then—or would have if they'd been born. And you *know* that today's really-really-long men's shorts that are worn off the ass are going to be the cause of much hilarity in the future, if they aren't already. In a decade or two, boys will risk being drummed right out of boy-dom if they dress that way. The other proof, at least in my own mind? Those photo spreads in *Entertainment Weekly* (a magazine I like) that show the best dresses at the latest awards show. I enjoy female beauty, so I gawk at them (after I read the movie reviews), and I think 75 percent of the dresses that get celebrated are awful. They make women I admire look like fabric pretzels.

I hasten to add that over the years I've mellowed in my view of fashion. At its best, I see it as an art form, doing what every art form does: producing a never-ending series of new creations, just for the sake of being able to enjoy them. Because novelty is fun. New designs are diverting. And beautiful clothes are . . . beautiful. This slant also helps explain why so much fashion is bad. The reason: in *any* art form, a lot of what is produced—maybe most of it—is bad. But some of it is good, and some of it is classic and never goes out of style. As witnessed by a recent issue of *Vanity Fair* that my loved one kindly placed in our bathroom. Who is on the cover? Grace Kelly.

What does still bother me, though, is the way a whole sub-population will subscribe to a way of looking that is obviously grotesque. You can supply your own examples I'm sure, but I have to mention women doing their eyes up like raccoons, and worst of all, women and men having work done on their faces so they no longer look like actual humans. This last trend shows how really dangerous is conformity. I saw a picture of Carol Burnett, a beloved comedienne, and I swear she looked like Bob Costas.

So there's a lot to be said for striking out on your own, and refusing to choose things just because the world endorses them. This applies especially to choosing a man.

Let's say there's a guy, Nick, who's interested in you; he approached you during happy hour, struck up a conversation, and was definitely making a play. Nick is a head turner, very stylish, six-foot-four, dark hair—like a more rugged Rob Lowe. He works in the financial industry. You've seen him three times now at the same bar and he has charmed the cynic right out of your girlfriends. One of these is Kristen, who has recently become a close ally of yours at work. Kristen is just wild about Nick. She is into fitness in a big way, and has got you working out with her, and she likes that Nick is ripped. Kristen will be really mad at you if you don't go after him— she's already acting like it's a fait accompli, planning the wedding, wanting to go on foursome trips. The last time you saw Nick, you sat at a table alone with him and the two of you had a long conversation. It went pretty well, though it seemed he was bringing most of the energy. He's definitely sexy. And undeniably handsome. But when you talk to him, you feel as if only part of you is engaged.

Then there's this other guy, Mr. Unlikely, you got to know accidentally through his job and yours, which overlap. You've taken to talking to him at the food wagon in the lobby. His name is Glen. He's got sandy receding hair, a slight belly, and big blue eyes that are not quite supported by the rest of his face, which features an irregular nose and a jaw that is not imposing. Oh, and he's the same height as you, not taller. But you love the way he smells, even when he has run down from the fifth floor, and his belly is firm (he's burly, not flabby). *GQ* isn't beating a path to his door, but you like his quirky way of honoring the dress code while always having a tie or belt or shirt that no one else would think of. Most of all, you like talking to him, because he seems to understand your stories almost better than you do, he offers anecdotes of his own that actually fit, and he laughs at the things you always thought were funny but no one else seemed to. When he's around, life seems more amusing and adversity easier to conquer. Okay, his face isn't conventionally handsome but, in your eyes, it works. You think he's cute. He tried to steal a kiss once when you went for a walk at lunchtime—actually, he did steal it—but you got awkward because you really hadn't decided whether you could wear him in public; but the kiss was good, it wanted to go on longer, it was starting something.

What do you do? Go with the easy choice, the instant shot of status that is Nick, and enjoy the ride? Write Glen off as an aberration because he isn't what "they" say is hot stuff? Or stick to your own guns and give him a chance?

I say go with Glen; give him your attention and explore things with him. To go with Nick is like buying the dress that is in, not the dress that is you.

One more light bulb about fashion and status. I said that slavishly following the new style is ultimately a form of conformity—people all trying to look a certain way because everybody else is trying to look that way. That actually hides individuals, absorbs them into sameness. Like Nick. Sure, he wears the latest trends, but isn't that just a way in which he is conforming to an external template? How does that get you any closer to knowing what makes him different and special? Maybe he isn't different and special.

The more people adhere to what society dictates, the more they become indistinguishable. Like those misled souls who have plastic surgery, so that they can all end up with the same face.

So shop for a guy who truly pleases you, not a guy you think will win the admiration of others. They aren't the ones who are going to have to love him.

7

old and improved

I don't know who invented the phrase "new and improved," but it has to be one of the most potent marketing slogans of all time. No doubt that's partly because it doesn't make sense. If the product has been improved, then it *isn't* new, it's the old peanut butter after all, with a few tweaks. But contradictions never stopped advertisers. "Sure, it's the same old peanut butter, but we've made it better, so it's NEW!" The implication is: you haven't already had this, no one has had this, you're on the cutting edge, you're getting virgin product, this isn't in any way used merchandise!

Did they inject it into us, or did they just take advantage of it, this restless craving for novelty that runs in our veins?

But you know what? Even "new" was getting kind of old, so the advertisers stepped in and improved it. Now it isn't enough to say something is new—they have to say it's ALL-NEW. Even if it's the latest episode of a TV drama. Were we really worried that they would mix in part of an old episode? Still, I for one have to say my life has been turned around. It's thrilling to get up every morning, not to a new day, but to an all-new day. I like to crack an all-new egg into my frying pan, and I don't mind washing it down with some all-new coffee.

No one is immune to this constant brainwashing. So when you head out to shop for a man, you may in some sense be unconsciously looking for an All-New Man. But what does this mean? There are several possibilities.

An all-new man could mean a guy you've never seen before.

Okay, that's cool. If you're unattached and looking, the best path to the man you want is to find a way to check out lots of guys you haven't met. Many of them. All-new guys. The wider the net you cast, the more likely the man you want is in it. The widest net is right there on your computer, and I'll be spotlighting it in this book, and getting down to the real practicalities of how you go from a new face on a screen to a partner who is sharing your life.

Once in a while, though, the face you want is not new; and that's worth thinking about too. Sometimes a guy you've already been with, maybe long ago, is the one. I keep hearing from couples who came across each other after years or decades. High-school friends who had crushes on each other but never acted on it, or were sweethearts and let it slip away when they went to college. They find each other years later—maybe they are now both divorced—and they get together and the same magic is there, only now it's sweeter. Facebook is making this happen a lot, by making it so easy to connect with long-lost friends.

Those are the exceptions that prove the rule. The best strategy is still to expose yourself to a generous crop of new men.

But there are also misguided forms of seeking the all-new man.

An all-new man could mean this week's model.

How about when your favorite man is the one you haven't had time to get used to (or tired of)? This isn't such a good way to go. If you insist on the blush of novelty, it means the guys you meet have an endangered shelf life. The guy you met last week is already losing his bloom, and the guy you meet tonight is a bad bet too, because in thirty days you'll have known him for a month. This may work well on a treasure hunt for sexual kicks, which is happening a lot today, at increasingly younger ages. If, however, you're looking for a relationship, it could get in the way.

The very nature of the shopping addiction is that the shirt we've worn once is somehow less thrilling, so we go out and find a shirt we haven't worn—or seen—before. But the very nature of a relationship is that it goes on for years, or a lifetime, and the new guy who thrills you is only going to work out if you'll still relish him when he isn't new. In fact, one of the most interesting challenges of checking out a promising guy is to see past the excitement of the present and peer through time at *the man he will be* when you've been together for years. Sound impossible? It isn't, as we'll see later.

The all-new man might be the man without a past.

Sounds like a movie title, but it's not a movie you want to be in.[1] The drive for the all-new can make you desire the man who seems unfettered by any annoying history. He is *so* new that he comes without attachments; it's as if he just arrived on the planet and you're going to get all of him because nobody else has had a nibble.

But slow down; it doesn't work that way.

_____

1. There is actually a movie with this title, a Finnish comedy-drama from 2002 about amnesia; but I'm not referring to it.

People without baggage, people who have managed a kind of Teflon passage through their lives so far, are going to show that Teflon to *you* some day. They're going to move on without a trace of you on them. Normal men with a heart and a soul have attachments, to family and friends, and they probably have romantic scars—at least one major love relationship that went wrong.

GLADDER AND WISER

And here is the good news, expressed in the finest advertising lingo: when you're shopping for a man, there's a lot to be said for the *old and improved*. Used is good. Avoid damaged merchandise, yes, but broken-in is good.

That's because men (and women) tend to become better partners with experience. People learn from failed relationships. Instead of sadder and wiser, these veterans of the romantic ring end up being Gladder and Wiser. (There I go again with an ad slogan.)

Why is this?

1. **They are no longer naive shoppers.** They have a better idea of what they're looking for. The guy you seek, maybe he bought for status last time, and he saw the error of that approach. So this time he's ready to trust his own preferences and tell the world to bug off. Which is why he's ready for you. Because you aren't some cookie-cutter model. You require a man who is in touch with his own taste.

2. **Gladder and wiser people learn to believe in themselves.** Rookies at love are apt to draw the wrong conclusion from failure or mistreatment. They think whatever happened is a

reflection on them—they take it personally: *Whatever the other person didn't like must be a flaw in me; it couldn't just be that they needed to be with someone else. (As did I.)*

But time heals this error, and you realize that you weren't a lousy conversationalist/lover, you just didn't like the other's way of talking/kissing. You didn't have a bad body, you just chose someone who liked another shape. You figure out that the way you're going to know the right partner is by the gusto with which they just naturally cotton to you in all your quirky glory. You rest on the bedrock of your own identity.

3. **The experienced folks know more about how to handle a worthy partner.** When relationships go belly-up, it's often because we were with the wrong people. But that isn't the whole story. Often we matched pretty well with our partner, but we made mistakes in how we treated them. One of the most common mistakes is making it too much about me and my needs. So we learn to love more unselfishly. We remember that we let someone feel neglected or hurt, or allowed them to be discouraged at a crucial time, and we decide not to let that happen again.

   Another mistake is being too willing to engage in hostilities, or too proud to back down. I talked about that earlier, how a failed relationship or two can make a body much more zealous about protecting the peace and not turning the other person into an opponent. We learn that goodwill is fragile, like a fine porcelain figure. We learn to cradle and protect it. And we bring down our metric on lag-time-before-apologizing.

So score one more for the thrift store: used can be better than new.

But how do you tell when the fellow in front of you has this value-added feature of being improved by experience? This will also be a topic in what follows, because in addition to peering into a man's future, you need to peer into his past—and there's a way to do it. Time travel isn't just a sci-fi marvel; it's also a crucial part of shopping.

8

shopping for someone
who is shopping for you

*U*sually when you shop, you are the shopper and the thing you want is the shoppee. It's a very clear-cut distinction. But when you're trying to secure a mate, you aren't making a unilateral "purchase." You're getting him, but he's also getting you. You're in a *reciprocal shopping* situation.

Now you might think that's bad news, because it's harder for two people to be pleased than just one. And maybe it *would* be easier if you could just go out and purchase a robot that was to your liking and had no demands of its own. You'd be kind of like the men in *The Stepford Wives* (1975), whose mates are turned into nubile automatons who simply serve their husbands. But although the movie mainly focuses on the wives' horrific fate, I'd have to say the husbands don't really seem to be getting such a good deal either. On either side, life with a completely passive partner could get a little deadly.

So let's look at the bright side of the mutual shopping situation. It means he's looking for you. So you have a shopping *ally*. He isn't just sitting in some remote cabin thinking, "I like serenity and seclusion. And maple syrup. I think I'll have some on my flapjack, before

I do some reading and reflect on the bliss of having no Internet." A guy like that could be very hard to find, even if the book he is reading is your favorite novel of all time.

Much better to envision a man who wakes up in his nifty apartment in town, and while checking his email he's thinking, "I'm gonna find her today." And he runs through his head a portrait of the woman he wishes was in his life, and although he doesn't know it yet, it's a portrait of you.

He thinks about her a lot, this woman who is you. And he tries to imagine where she works, and where she goes when she's not at work, what she likes to do, and what he could do to close the gap between him and . . . you.

So that's a huge advantage to you as a shopper. Imagine if your perfect party dress was out on the streets, watching for you, or getting online and trying to find you—wouldn't shopping be a whole lot easier? But that's what this guy is all about!

Now, he may be pretty hard to please, and you probably are too, but that's not bad news. That's not going to make things harder, it's going to make them easier. Because the two of you have one fabulous characteristic. You are the people perfectly designed to please each other.

Where do I get such a giddily optimistic assumption?[1]

You may well ask. Because you may be discouraged about finding such a fitting man, especially since you haven't found him yet. My reply is simple: **Optimism makes a better shopper.** You have a better chance of finding the shoes you need for that gallery opening

---

1. An earlier book of mine, *Why Mr. Right Can't Find You*, was called "giddily optimistic" in a review in *Publishers Weekly*—a very kind review, by the way. I think optimism is effective when you face what you're up against and find a way through. I'm not sure if it's giddy, though there could be a little vertigo when you realize that you really can find a good partner, and certainly later when you find them.

if you believe they're out there. It improves your vision, makes you look harder, and makes you ready to try something a little different.

And really, it's a pretty reasonable assumption. You're a gifted, attractive person with a good heart. Why *wouldn't* there be a terrific guy out there among the millions of single men, who could make magic with you? The only thing that used to make this hard to prove (say, until the year 2000) was that you only got to look at a tiny sample of available and desirable men. You couldn't cast a wide enough net. But now you can. Problem solved; proof forthcoming in Part Four.

So it's better to decide right now that there is someone out there whose wish list describes you, and vice versa. You'll have a lot easier time shopping if you picture him out there. Let me expand on this crucial point, starting with a chapter title which is itself expansive.

9

portray the man you seek

paint him to yourself so he becomes real to you
and you can more easily connect with him

*B*ack before cell phones, studies showed that people are able to find each other even when they can't communicate, by employing a kind of "collaboration at a distance." An example would be where two friends are separated while exploring a foreign city (and haven't yet got accommodations). They have a better chance of finding each other if they each focus on the fact that the other person is trying to find them and is thinking along with them, trying to "agree" on a prominent, no-brainer meeting spot that they are both aware of, and which both of them are likely to be able to locate.

Similarly, when you start picturing a specific man who is out there looking for you and who believes you are looking for him, you both suddenly have a better shot at connecting with each other. Before I go into the reasons why, let me say something about *how* you think of him.

Don't just imagine a specimen; imagine a relationship.

There are things we can enjoy about someone even when that person isn't actively relating to us. We can enjoy their physical features from across the room. Their pale coloring, their bright eyes, their lustrous hair, the graceful way they walk, the melody of their voice, the playful smile they give to someone else. We can enjoy how smart they are, listening to them talk on the phone to a friend, or watching them deal with a crisis that doesn't involve us. We can get pleasure out of the clothes they wear and the way they look when they're taking their clothes off. We can dig their touch with a cat or a car, their way with an omelet or a bassoon. That is the kind of thing I mean by seeing another person as a *specimen*. It is what they are apart from us: what they would be even if we weren't in the picture. But if you concentrate only on those things, even if you make sure (as I recommended) to paint a picture that speaks to your own original tastes, you will omit half the person you seek.

Because there is going to be another dimension to your partner: the part of him that only happens when you are in the picture. Not so much what he is in himself, but what the two of you create. Meaning what sparks fly when you interact, what kind of music you make together. So when you're composing a mental picture of your guy, write yourself some scenes for two.

Write a character whose company you are going to enjoy for years; a man you will want to share activities with even when you're older; a guy you are going to like a lot, for a long time. Some day when you've gotten over the initial infatuation, it may be nice to sit with him in a restaurant and tell yourself, he sure is handsome, and fit, and successful, and masterful; but it'll be a whole lot nicer if you have something to say to each other. And it will do no good to admire him if you can't open up to him emotionally, and have him open up to you. Although externals may be very eye-catching at the beginning, internals are going to matter more as time goes by, and eventually you won't be able to tell the difference, because every overt feature of your partner will be a manifestation of the person you know him to be.

Don't let the shopping analogy take you in a shallow direction; don't simply portray your future partner as one very glossy hunk of merchandise. Think of him as a soul that dances better when it dances with you.

So go crazy and picture in detail the things you will delight in doing together. To prime your imagination, here are a few examples of things actual couples share:

- **Outings:** these could be anything from a cruise around town to a drive in the country to a vacation trip. Many couples enjoy these excursions more than they have any right to, because when they take off from the stresses of home and work, they rediscover an almost childish delight in each other. Think about the top five outings you would hope to enjoy with your partner, from the frivolous to the profound.

- **Stories:** when you live with someone, it's inevitable that you spend a lot of time reporting to each other on the things that happen to you while you're apart. Like what kind of day you just had. If you care about each other's experiences, and both enjoy the other's narrative style, you are off to the races. Hint: a lot of this depends on whether you each process experiences—and people—in a way that the partner finds compelling. Especially people. What stories do you most like to tell, and what stories would you most like to hear from a guy?

- **Activities:** here's a story. Chase and Gina were schoolteachers. One taught special-needs kids, the other didn't. They fell in love, married, and adopted two children, one of whom was a serious handful. During the summers, Gina spent time working at an old hotel in Martha's Vineyard, and Chase stayed home with the kids. Finally, after some challenging years, they got to the empty nest phase, and soon after that, they retired. And here is the interesting part. Instead of a time to take it easy, this stage was the reward that had got them through the tough times. They were both elated because, much as they loved their children and teaching, they were free to be a couple again and spend time together. The crowning touch was that they could finally do what they'd been wanting to do all those years: hike the Appalachian Trail, all 2,174 miles from Mount Katahdin in Maine to Springer Mountain in Georgia. They had crewed on the Trail sometimes, working with eclectic groups of volunteers on arduous projects like building shelters and relocating paths. But they hadn't hiked it. This was their dream: to be together again, with fewer responsibilities and enough money saved, to be able to continue where their pre-parenting years had left off.

- **Sex:** we certainly can't leave this one out of a list of ways you want to connect. But let's make it broader. What forms of sensuality do you want to share with your love-muffin? Do you want him to like cuddling? Giving and receiving massage? Foot rubbing? What is your definition of a good kisser?[1] What is your agenda in bed? (Different people put the emphasis on different areas.) Do

---

1. In *Why Mr. Right Can't Find You* I wrote in detail about the two kinds of good kisser who wander this earth, and how awkward it can be when one kind has an oral encounter with the other. Hint: it has a lot to do with how the tongue is used, and how early it is deployed. For juicy details, please see that book.

you want to get theatrical? Do you want kinky? Is basic chemistry more important to you than Olympic stats? All answers are right, as long as you find someone who agrees with them.

Using these examples as a jumping-off point, make a list of some of the things you would hope to enjoy with your partner—the ways you will "get it on" with each other that will give your life together a healthy sizzle. Resolve as a shopper that you're not going to look just at what he is in himself; you're going to look for *connections* between you, in as many dimensions as possible. If you think that way from the get-go, you are less likely to wind up with a man who is a great "catch" but doesn't float your boat.

Bonus point: The more clearly you envision him, the easier it'll be for you to eliminate guys who *couldn't be him*. And every time you do that, you're one step closer to him.

What do you already know about the right guy? Let's start with this: he's your ally—he's looking for *you*. Remember my giddily optimistic statement that you two are perfectly designed to please each other? It can bear big dividends right now. Because one thing it means is, he isn't going to find you wanting in any major ways. If you hold fast to this principle, you will be strong and secure in your search. You'll know that any guy who picks holes in you isn't the right guy. And you'll walk on, bidding him a cheerful "Good luck."

In other words, *shop for someone who likes what you are*. Let's take body type as an example. Of all the counsel I've given, the point that has been greeted the most joyfully by women is this: you don't have to change your natural physical type in order to appeal to the guy you're looking for; and if a man wants you to change it, he isn't the right guy for you.

Of course it's good to be healthy and fit, and to be at a weight that is consistent with those two things. But that doesn't in any way mean you have to conform to a stereotype that nature never intended for you. Yet many women—maybe most women—believe that they are defective. (As do increasingly many men, for similar reasons.) The average size of an adult woman in the United States is a fourteen, and many of these women are healthy and fit and attractive, as are many larger-sized women. But the average size shown in magazines and on TV is more like a four. Could it be that someone is making a profit off convincing people that they are not alright? Obviously it could. We have the multibillion-dollar weight-loss industry, and we have plastic surgeons, and there is the general tendency of television to make you feel you aren't okay in so many ways, and you aren't as cool as the people on the screen—that's how they hook you as a viewer, and induce you to buy their products.

But this is a shopper's guide to men, and men don't adhere to somebody else's notion of what is attractive. Well, some of them do, but they are wusses who are afraid of offending their peer group, or they are buying for status—making the rash assumption that what the world approves of must be what they want. In either case they are being cheated if they suppress their own tastes.

Most men have a visceral response to a woman they like, and it isn't determined by fashion despots in Paris or by TV directors. And there is no such thing as a female body type that "most men" want. Men are not uniform in their tastes. Roughly 40 percent of men prefer a slender woman. Roughly 40 percent of men prefer a full-figured woman.[2] Lots of men don't really care. They are more than happy if a

---

2. A *Times Mirror* 1990 Body Image Survey is typical; it reports that 44 percent of men prefer women with generous figures and 42 percent like women who are thin.

body is anatomically female and has a tendency to offer itself to them when the mood is right, and they like the person it belongs to. Some men and some women have more particular tastes, and that's fine too as long as they please each other.

As one reader eloquently put it after reading my take on this issue: "I am valuable and fabulous exactly the way I am. I don't need to be skinnier, heavier, taller, shorter, have larger hips or boobs, smaller hips or boobs, longer eyelashes or fuller lips." Spurred on by this realization that the man she sought would dig her just as she was, this woman found a great relationship, which is still going strong.

Body type is just one example. The same point applies to faces. Different people are moved by different faces and find beauty, or humanity, or something simpatico in them. And minds are no different. The takeaway here is that if you approach the finding of a man with a sense of deficiency, you will end up in a deficient relationship. It is immensely liberating and empowering, for women *and* men, to realize that the someone who is out there looking for you is going to relish you in a whole lot of ways, will be awed by how fabulous you are, will think they are so lucky to have found you.

You have to believe in that guy, have to believe in the bond that you and he will share and the pleasure you will both find in your future union, in order to sweep aside the wannabes who aren't right for you and avoid giving in to a half-hearted rapport. Or worse, installing a critic in your life. You are not shopping for a critic who will disparage you and undermine your self-esteem. Or a skeptic who will doubt your best impulses and dampen your brightest talents. If you know this in advance, really know it, you will find it strangely easy and painless to navigate past the wrong men until you find the one with whom you will catch the wind and fly.

10

love you can afford

*U*nlike many things you shop for, you can probably only accommodate one of these man-things at a time, maybe only one in a lifetime.

So you want to get a good one. Yet you don't want to overreach and go for somebody who is beyond your means, and end up paying for the rest of your life.

When you're unattached and looking, you're going to run into two types of people who don't fit your budget:

- people you want but who don't return your interest (you can't afford them)

- people who want you but you aren't interested enough in them (they can't afford you)

Let's take each of these situations in order, then we'll get to the one that lies between them.

Someone who doesn't return your interest

It is rude of life to throw this at us. It's a terrible indignity, but we all sometimes develop a hankering for someone who doesn't seem to hanker in return. If you try hard enough, you may secure the purchase, but you will be paying forever. Put another way, you'll give more than you'll get, and you'll keep on giving.

Here are a couple of shapes this guy may take.

The casual wolf. Especially when you're young, it's easy to be lured and beguiled by the most elusive guy in the pack, especially if he perversely gives you just enough encouragement to get you on the hook.

You keep seeing that wavy-haired rogue at the club, the one who is always laughing with other people but sometimes looks at you with intention in his pale eyes. If you take the bait, later he turns into the guy who is dating you but is non-committal about who else he's dating, and one of your girlfriends saw him with another girl last night after he left your place. He is really good in bed, and reaches you in ways you can't even fathom, and you miss him when you don't see him for a while, but he doesn't seem to have a problem with that. In fact, he seems very easy about the whole thing, never worried, never bothered about his hold on you or whether he could lose you. His heart is as unruffled as his leather jacket and the smooth purr of his car.

Cool is glamorous, but it's a bad bargain. Even a vampire is no good to you if he doesn't sometimes get breathless with passion, just as debilitated with longing as you are.

So much for the wolf who is too offhand about your heart. But there's another kind of user who tends to crop up a little later in life, and also skimps on the emotion you deserve.

The sheep in wolf's clothing. This is the guy who wants to be just friends. He's great company, he's still good looking (though slightly running to seed), and he shares feelings with you that make you think you're really close to him. He tells you how proud he is of his daughter and gets tears in his eyes. He even wants you to join his family for dinner when they're in town. And once in a blue moon he kisses you, but then he acts kind of awkward, almost as if he was out of line—like you were his sister or something.

On the evenings when he gets a little physical, or a lot emotional, you know you're falling in love with him.

But you can't afford him. Not because he's too good for you. No, it's because he isn't *interested enough* in you. He may be super-duper or he may be unexceptional, but for whatever reason, he is not sufficiently struck by your merit.

So the worst thing that could happen to you would be to somehow win him. That would only result in you giving too much, contributing more than your share, while he lounges in the comfort of your love. You wouldn't receive the passion that you deserve. That's a bad bargain. You'd be like a woman who works three jobs to keep paying the interest on a house that was too expensive in the first place.

Maybe this guy could be an ardent wolf with somebody else. Maybe he could be a passionate, giving partner. It doesn't matter, because he isn't fit for you.

The guy who leaves you lukewarm

Then we have the other pole, where you have a guy after you in a big way but you are lukewarm. When you're unattached and lonely, and have some spare time to kill, it can be very tempting to while away some of it with a guy like this, hoping you'll find Mr. Right farther down the road. For one thing, it's good for your ego. But it isn't kind. You'd be doing the same thing to him as the wolf/sheep we just looked at tried to do to you. And you'd be stuck with a guy who is always trying to earn a better grade that you can't give him. Or makes you feel like you have a stingy heart. That's not how you want to feel.

Which brings us to the Goldilocks moment: when the other person doesn't want you too *much* (so it's overwhelming) or too *little* (so it's draining); they want you with just the right fervency. Yay!

THE SIX DIMENSIONS OF AFFINITY

It's really about the appeal that two people hold for each other that makes each one want to "have" the other. It's an equal magnetic force, a balance in charisma let's call it. And when you find it, it will have six dimensions, this mutual appreciation, regard, or relishing.

- **Sex:** you not only want each other's bods, but you develop a hunger for what each other's bods do in bed. As I said earlier, you appreciate the terrain that you're able to share, sexually and sensually.[1]

- **Desire:** this includes sex, but it goes beyond it to a yearning to be with that person, a feeling on both sides that one's life must have them in it and that one wants them as a partner. At first this yearning may be hot and romantic, but later it will become a slow-burning, constant flame called *attachment*.

---

1. Sex is an activity and I mentioned it as such in the previous chapter, but it's also a powerful magnetic force that pulls you toward someone.

- **Admiration:** it's great to admire your partner, in fact it's essential. But he has to admire you too. There are going to be times when he takes your breath away and you are in awe of him, and feel deliciously unworthy. But at least as often—*more* often would be acceptable—the pendulum should swing the other way, and you should catch him looking at you with googly eyes, and feel perfectly deserving of such worship.

- **Interest:** we are all interesting when seen with the right eyes. Choose someone who gets you. And you him. Someone whose thoughts would interest you even if you were just reading them in a blog and didn't know him.

- **Respect:** it's good for both of you to be just a little afraid of the other person. Afraid of disappointing them, afraid of hurting them, afraid of being unworthy of them. That way you don't trifle with them or take them for granted. Being with them is a form of practicing respect for every human.

- **Entertainment value:** it don't mean a thing if it ain't got that zing. If it isn't fun to be together, if it isn't frequently a fine form of entertainment, something is wrong. You should look forward to spending time with this person. They should get a lift when they're having a bad day and you walk into the room.

That's the balance you're looking for—two boats pulling equally toward each other, in all those ways. (I'll talk about tracking these dimensions of affinity when we get to the trial period.)

You may be wondering why I don't put love on this list. It's hovering all around it. But love is mystical and elusive, hard to measure—an *x* quantity. Even when we love our partner deeply, we don't always feel it on a conscious level, but it grows over time, it bridges time, and sometimes it hits home to us with amazing, poignant force and we know we're in the grip of it. The dimensions I've listed above are more down to earth and easier to get a reading on, and they all confirm that a real love is in prospect. Call them aspects of love if you wish.

Being "in love," by the way, is a whole other animal. Two people can be utterly smitten, and equally smitten, and yet totally unsuited to each other. Infatuation comes and goes like a fickle breeze, and can merrily lead people into disastrous couplings. When it happens to well-matched people, it is a wonderful gateway to intimacy and a first step toward the real thing, and when you meet the right person, it will very probably happen to you. I'll have a lot more to say about it in Part Five.

Why sex is the odd man out. And now, a special note about sex. I nonchalantly grouped it with the other five dimensions of affinity. But it is different. It travels solo, and they go in a group.

Sexual desire is the joker in the deck. It's the only card that has little to do with whether you value someone as a human being. This is the major conundrum in the quest for a mate, maybe the biggest monkey wrench in the works. You can find a guy whom you admire, find interesting, respect, and enjoy hugely, and let's even throw in that he has major lust for you, and yet you don't find him sexually attractive or don't like his sexual style/agenda. Or conversely: you may have the hots for a dude who doesn't impress you in other ways. Worse than that, you may like a man on every level including sex and yet *he* doesn't feel a physical attraction.

It shouldn't be that way. Life would be a whole lot easier if sincere affection automatically produced sexual desire, at least toward unattached members of whatever gender you favor. Then a lot more people would qualify for being your partner—which would help the odds of finding said prize.

No such luck. So when you're shopping for a mate, the situation is complicated by the fact that you're shopping for two diverse kinds of attraction: sexual, and all-the-rest. The non-sexual areas are rational and have more to do with friendship; they spring from your values and goals, what you're working at and what you enjoy, where you're heading, and who you are as a person. Yet you also have to check for this other thing, this stirring in the loins, which is non-rational and also has to be felt on both sides.

What is a girl to do? You have to keep your head and admit that sex is not the same thing as friendship, and don't be swept away by sexual chemistry: don't let it make you think the guy is your soulmate. But don't underrate it (I didn't think you would!), because it has an amazing, transformative gift to bring. It works a kind of alchemy, altering the ingredients that would make someone your friend so that they turn him into your partner. Sex itself gets transmuted by this process: it becomes a way of expressing love, though it still carries its trademark physical charge.

One of the good things about meeting men in the real world (as opposed to online) is that you can usually tell pretty quickly whether there is any physical attraction. (You can certainly tell if there's a *lack* of reaction in this area.) So you don't have to bark up the tree of romance with a dude, only to discover down the line that he belongs in the friend neck of the woods. The non-sexual areas take longer to explore—a much greater investment of time. So it's nice to have a heads-up about which men to explore them with.

A love you can afford is a love that is firing on all six cylinders, for both of you. In all these ways you feel your man voting Yes on you, and you return the favor. It's a spectrum of affinity that plays a big part in making two people go the distance.

PART
THREE

LET'S SHOP!

11
shop, and always shop

$\mathcal{D}$ecember rolled around and I saw my spouse at her desk doing things with wrapping paper. I said, "How's your Christmas shopping going?" She has a lot of people to whom she likes to give presents, so I couldn't imagine she could be finished.

She said, "Done. Got my cards too."

I had not even started, thanks to a long-time habit. When I was in high school I would go out on Christmas Eve and buy a book or a record for each member of my family, then go home and wrap same (usually in newspaper, circled by a red ribbon). Since then I have grown as a human being, so I tend to head out *two* days before Christmas and buy for my true love something culinary, something decorative, and maybe if I'm feeling reckless, something to wear. And it isn't easy. Because when you shop at the last minute you may not find anything you really like. If panic sets in, you may fail to see what is right in front of you.

This much I knew, but what I learned from my partner is that there's a better way. That is to shop all the time, always be aware of items you're seeing that might be just the ticket. That's what she does: she wanders through the world, things catch her eye, and she grabs them because they'd be perfect for so-and-so. If occasionally that so-and-so is herself, who can fault her?

She knows what smart shoppers know: if you don't grab it when you see it, it may not be there when you realize you want it or get up the guts to spring for it. The store may run out of your size, and not be able to reorder. Or the manufacturer may stop making it—this happened to me with an amazing pair of equipment sandals that I was too foolish to buy when I first tried them on. Adidas stopped making them.

Just yesterday I pulled this off again. Two months ago I had seen a remarkable hat in a friend's store, a summer hat made by Dorfman Pacific with a wide brim, partially surfaced in mesh to let the breeze through but able to block the sun's rays. The perfect hat to wear while walking for exercise or strolling for amusement. On top of that, it was a cool shade of green, had a leather chin cord to secure it against the wind, and it came in an extra-large so it could fit gracefully on my jumbo head. Like I said, it was in a friend's store so I could also get a real good price on it. So of course I didn't buy it. What I did was feel smug about having such a fine purchase in my future, and resolve to get my main squeeze to view it on me, to make sure it wasn't one of those hats that make me look dumb. (Of which there are many. I had a straw hat once that I liked, and it was so bad that my friend refused to paddle in the bow of our canoe if I wore it in the stern, and he was facing *frontward*.)

So yesterday I brought her to the store and they had five of these hats left, but the extra-large was gone, and they couldn't order just one hat. I was heartbroken because shopping isn't easy for me and this was lined up to be a shopping triumph. Yes, I looked online, for an hour. No, it isn't there.

The moral of these stories is: **Shop all the time**, and when you see a good one, make your move. What's weird is that men follow the rule only with regard to women, and women follow it *except* regarding men. (More about men's methods in a moment.)

But a chance sighting of someone who could really be your life partner is so rare and so precious that it needs to be acted on. It's like spying a fine carving in a curio shop in Morocco: you may never see it again, so you better do something now.

Do I believe in love at first sight? Well, I believe that you can detect a whole lot about someone when you first set eyes on them: not just whether you find them attractive, but also whether you like their style and their attitude, whether they are fit or not, healthy or not, conservative or bohemian, whether they have a corporate vibe or seem of freer stock. And whether they are interested in you. All this can move you a considerable distance toward qualifying them as a candidate worth exploring. When you go ahead and explore, you sometimes find out fairly quickly that you're on the wrong track, for example if they tell you that *Real Bachelors of Nebraska* is their favorite TV show. But sometimes the dominoes keep falling and an encounter like this leads to the real thing, and looking back on it, you can't be blamed if you say it was love at first sight.

Okay, when it comes to women, men just naturally follow the adage that it's better to be always looking. Let's take advantage of that. Let's have a look at how your dream man conducts himself in his search for you. That will help you help him. We'll stay in the real world for a while, where human mating started out, and see what goes down on its well-trodden streets. Then we'll turn to the Internet, where shopping ceases to be a metaphor and different tactics are called for.

12

imagine the shopping situation
he's in and cater to it

We agreed that a worthy beast is out there looking for you. Here's another benefit of that realization: you can figure out how to make his challenge a little easier. Let's make a few notes on how he shops for you, and how he imagines you might shop for him—or *wishes* you *would* shop for him. We'll calibrate your moves to his, until the two of you collide in a wild embrace.

The simplest way to say this is, figure out where he's searching and go there in a nice chemise.

Okay, how *does* a man search for you? In the living, breathing world (as opposed to online), he does it by constantly being alert to women he hasn't seen before—that roving eye we hear so much about. On a primitive level, his eyes are programmed to seek out that which his loins could and would impregnate. Because evolution rewards procreation. On a more civilized, "nice guy" level, your modern unattached and somewhat lonely, eligible, and mighty desirable male keeps looking around, thinking, "If I can just run across her, and strike up a conversation with her, won't that be holy high jinks."

As he treads the streets of the city, does he make a clever plan and deliberately walk where you are likely to be? Well he would, but these things are unpredictable. One moment you're in the supermarket, the next you're at the gym, then a restaurant, then home, then work . . . The problem is, he doesn't *know* where you'll be. So he mostly sticks to his usual beat and hopes your paths will cross, because he does go to many of the same places a woman goes.

Now, it's true there are places where more women go than men, and there he would have a better shot at you. Especially if the place was relaxed and sociable, conducive to striking up a conversation, a place of leisure let us say. How about women's departments in stores? Cruise the women's clothing aisles and sure enough, you will see lots of solo women. But somehow this doesn't recommend itself to your average guy. He's afraid he'll be taken as some kind of opportunist-stalker, or as a guy who's into women's clothing. And based on shopping with his ex-girlfriend, he wonders if a woman will be in a mood to be approached (his ex was often a bit testy while shopping). Also, there's no place to sit, no refreshments, and bad lighting.

How about art galleries? More girls than boys go to them, right? But strangely enough, people tend to do this more when they're visiting a city they don't live in. As tourists we all suddenly become mad about art, hungry for historical details. But he wants to meet a girl who lives in his city. Okay, that's not his real objection. His real hesitancy is that he's afraid of being caught as a poseur, pretending a passion or expertise he doesn't have. He may run into a gal who's very serious about art and who wants the same in a guy. And again, there's a kind of reverent atmosphere in a gallery that doesn't encourage one to accost a complete stranger and engage in chitchat.

But what if he *is* into art in a serious way? That suggests another avenue a man can use—if he has any specialized hobby or pastime.

BOUTIQUE SHOPPING

When you have pursued some activity or interest to the point where it becomes a second calling, you're going to meet others who do the same thing.

Ted was a carrot-headed guy who came out of a difficult divorce with a woman whose moods were darker and stormier than his. He had by then gotten heavily into dancing—ballroom and other—but he didn't have a regular partner. One day at a club he saw a girl in motion on the floor and told himself, "Now *she* can dance." That led, fairly quickly, to love and marriage and little red-headed dancers.

It's the boutique version of mate shopping. It can happen with any serious hobby, from rock climbing to dog showing to choral singing. For your future man and for you, this is a great way to be exposed to people—some of them unattached—who already share a core interest with you and are therefore that much more likely to be compatible. The nice thing is, most of us already have this in motion; we already have special activities that we love to engage in. And we do meet new people through them, so it's an excellent place to have your mate-shopping antennae on high alert. Not only that, but it's usually very easy to strike up a conversation with anyone in the group, because that's what people are there to do.

While we're on the subject, Meetup.com is a resource that you don't want to overlook. Many of us have interests that we pursue alone, and we'd like to share them with others and get reinforcement and a chance to learn more. Meetup is an international online facility for making this happen on a local level. It makes it easy for people in the same region who have a common passion to find each other, and when they reach critical mass, form a group and start getting together. Whether you want the athletic or the spiritual, the outdoorsy or the café-ish, you can find like-minded people who want to hike, play softball, meditate, write songs, ride motorcycles, play chess, watch indie movies, or just bitch about life. So join a Meetup group or start one, just for the sake of that activity you want to pursue, and the bonus is, it will bring new people to you who share that interest, some of them being unattached men.

Boutique shopping is a cool approach, and your dream man hopes to encounter you that way. But still, most of the time he finds himself in the wider world. Let's see where that can lead. He goes about his daily round, and he keeps a watch for anyone who could be you. And he hopes you will do that too: he hopes you will realize that *wherever you are, he might be there*. Simple as it may sound, this is the number one favor you as a shopper can do for him as a shopper.

So when you're in the drugstore and you observe a nice-looking, non-ring-wearing guy stealing glances at you, don't assume he's confused about allergy medicines and thinks you may be an expert, since you are not sneezing. Assume that he may admire you for some other reason than your lack of symptoms; and since you already think he's attractive, give this moment a chance. Don't worry that you were shopping for toothpaste, not a man. Don't worry that you didn't dress with this agenda in mind. (You've already attracted his shopping eye.) Don't be too structured and professional. Not all good moments are planned. Give serendipity a chance.

How do you give it a chance? You run this mantra through your head:

- If I don't meet some men, I won't meet the one I'm looking for.

- This guy looks kind of meetable. He seems to be noticing me, and I like the look of him.

- Maybe I should encourage him somehow, so that we might perhaps converse with one another.

But how do you encourage him—how do you rouse the rakish rogue? Before my first book was even published, a journalist friend of mine read the manuscript and reported excitedly to me, "I tried your Smile Technique last night in a bookstore and it worked! We're going on a date!" It took me a minute to realize what she meant, because I wasn't aware that I had pioneered a new technique in the great tradition of the Heimlich maneuver and the Brandt-Daroff Exercises.[1] I thought I had said, when you notice an interesting guy being interested in you, try smiling at him. Most men don't want to look overly aggressive and they aren't always brave, especially when they see a woman they really admire, so he may not approach you if you don't give him a hint that he wouldn't be unwelcome. So overcome that reflex training that makes you avoid eye contact with any man you haven't met, and give him a smile. Then he is very likely to make the "first" move. If he doesn't, you have lost nothing.

That was the gist of it. When my friend called it a "technique" I was taken aback, because I wasn't recommending some clever new maneuver. To me a smile was a natural thing, old as love, and it could convey a timely message that would make a man braver.

However you look at it, it works.

One other note: be especially alert to possible encounters when you are in a place that reflects your unique values, like an organic food store or a music club where your favorite unsigned band is playing.

---

1. The Brandt-Daroff Exercises are a series of rapid lying-downs, sitting-ups, and head-turnings that help lessen a type of vertigo.

So far we've been looking mainly at chance meetings, which are indeed full of promise and are extremely underexploited by mate shoppers everywhere. But there is another way. I said earlier that you and your future man can collaborate at a distance and help each other end up in the same place. And sometimes his mind heads down that track.

He fantasizes about how you might think about him. He wishes you would imagine the things that go through his head. Then you could figure out what we said before, that he might not go to women's departments looking for you, even though there are concentrations of solo women there. But there's a place he knows about, where there are lots of unattached men and not many solo women, so if you went there, you could probably talk to any guy you wanted to, and one of those guys might be him. It's also a comfortable place with refreshments, and it's a sociable spot. He has often sat there alone, in the late afternoon when the sun was slanting in the door, or in the evening, and wished that you would walk in. Because it would be so easy for you to catch each other's eye and start talking.

He wishes you would realize all that and go there in a nice chemise.

I'm talking of course about a bar—a pub, or a nice restaurant-bar. I raised a fair rumpus when I said in *Why Mr. Right Can't Find You* that women should go to bars alone. I meant, of course, what I call "conversation bars," as opposed to noisy, dangerous, or meat-market joints. The plain fact is that many desirable guys go to a pub alone, just to get a glass of draft beer and to while away an hour or so, and they are very accessible and few solo women are around.

The women who do come in are either with a man or with other women. The former will obviously discourage interested guys, but what's not always understood is that the latter will too. The average guy is much less likely to approach a woman who is in a group of women, or even with one other woman. It's bad enough to risk rejection by one female, but to have to pass muster with two or five is worse. Again, having your opening line scrutinized by one woman (whom you already admire enough to approach) is daunting enough, but having it critiqued by a committee is over the top. Reverse the situation and ask yourself, if you were in a bar, would you be more likely to approach a group of men or a guy on his own? When they're in groups, both genders tend to form a kind of hormone-soaked pha-lanx that's a little hard for a solo member of the opposite sex to tangle with.

Ergo, because most women commonly seen in nice bars are not solo, they are not approachable. Therefore it's a buyer's market if you're willing to be a solo female. And buyer's markets are good for shoppers. As I said in the earlier book, bars are crawling with Mr. Rights.

If you want all the reasons for my stance, plus my answers to the misgivings some women expressed, I refer you to that book. But here's the main point, with new evidence. The most powerful engine for meeting a great partner is still online dating. But sometimes you've spent all day at a computer. You don't want to sit at a screen— you want to go out in the real world, be brave and intrepid, feel the old adrenaline pulsing, and do some shopping the old-fashioned way, by moving your feet. And in that case, the easiest, most likely way to meet a nice guy is in a conversation bar.

I keep hearing this view confirmed by women, in emails from readers who have tried it and succeeded, and even when I'm being interviewed. One journalist was asking me questions for a newspaper article, and when we got to the part about going to bars, she said she doubted that her readers would believe a serious relationship could begin there, much less that they would go to a bar solo. I said, "Well, if that's too hard, you could go with a girlfriend, but then my maxim is, the one who isn't alone should approach the one who is." There was an odd silence from her and then we went on to other topics— like a new guy she'd met whom she was very excited about. Before meeting him she had not dated for quite a while and she was full of questions about how to nurture this new connection, as well as obviously euphoric about him and just wanting to share. And then in an almost guilty tone she blurted out something that made me laugh. She said, "Okay, I have to say it. I met him in a pub; I went there with a girlfriend and he was sitting alone at the bar, and he kept looking at me, and I thought he was cute. Oh, and I spoke to him first. You were right about everything."

"What did you say?" (I'm interested in opening lines; I'm convinced they don't have to be very clever when the vibe is right.)

"I asked him what he was eating. We started talking and I invited him over to our table. We made a date that night."

You won't necessarily find true love when you go to a conversation bar, but you will very likely meet some nice men and that's the first step. All the shopping tips in this book should go with this reminder: **You're not gonna find the right guy on the first outing, but if you check out *lots* of nice guys, you'll get there.**

SHOPPING SOLO

If you are like most women, you often shop by your lonesome when you're hunting for clothing or a new food processor or a hammock. But somehow, when it's time to go out and expose yourself to the hungry hearts of men, that independence is MIA. You think you need the moral support of another single female, or better yet, a group of them. Maybe that's because a companion proves you aren't really looking for a guy, or that you aren't "desperate for love" since you have at least one friend. Whereas if you venture alone, say into a bar, that must immediately brand you as one of society's unfortunates, a languisher, a castaway somehow missed by the currents of desire and affection. Why don't you feel this way about shopping alone for a pair of shoes? Why aren't you afraid of being grouped with the shoe-less hoards who prey on boats from Italy?

It has to be because of what you're shopping *for*, not that you're shopping alone. As if there was something uniquely embarrassing about shopping for a man. As if this is a need you simply shouldn't have.

There are lots of reasons why you might feel this way, but I think the deepest one comes from a very traditional, and outdated, place. The belief is, romance should *come to* a woman; she shouldn't have to seek it out. If it doesn't happen for her by the age of, say, twenty-seven, then there is something very wrong, and anything that exposes that fact to the light of day, or the woody glow of a tavern, only compounds the shame!

It's okay to shop for shoes or a new bedspread, because they aren't supposed to seek a woman out and beg for her hand. But a man? That's different.

We have this on solid authority. An ancient tale says it all, one that is fed to young girls along with their bedtime cookie and takes root in the susceptible girlish brain. It is so familiar and so strange that we will take a little romp through it in the very next chapter, and turn it on its lovely head.

Meanwhile, let's remember that this idea of the woman waiting passively to be approached came from a time when people lived in villages and towns and everybody knew everybody; the eligible bachelors knew exactly who the local bachelorettes were, and so a smitten swain could indeed approach his preferred damsel at a special event held for that purpose, called a dance.

But we live in vast sprawling urban landscapes, where the guy who needs to be yours goes to one Burger King and you go to another, and he doesn't have a clue where you are. He can't take a stroll on the village common and view the local maidens serving pork pies.

That is why it is not embarrassing for you to toss your hat into the ring and say, "I am looking for someone, I want to meet a good man."

It is not embarrassing—it is essential.

13

the sleeping beauty syndrome

fairy tale as bad self-help text

Of all the myths that discourage you from proactively shopping for a good mate, the premier one is this: *True Love only happens to the woman who doesn't seek it out. If she will just wait, the perfect man will ride into her life. (Or if he doesn't, she never could have found true love anyway.)*

This myth is perfectly encapsulated in the fairy tale we know as "Sleeping Beauty." Honored in book, ballet, and film, it provides the ultimate *bad* role model for a woman who wants to find a lifetime partner.[1] Let's look at the ingredients of that strangely seductive tale.

A banquet is held to celebrate the birth of a princess. Fairies give her various gifts: she shall be the most beautiful, the most gracious, and so on. But the newborn princess is cursed by a jealous fairy who

---

1. A story called "The Sleeping Beauty in the Wood" was part of Charles Perrault's *Stories or Tales from Times Past; or, Tales of Mother Goose,* published in France in 1697. Perrault's version of the story has its roots in Giambattista Basile's tale, "Sun, Moon, and Talia," published in Italy in 1674, and in even earlier folktales. The Brothers Grimm weighed in with two versions of the story, "Little Briar-Rose" and "The Glass Coffin" (1812). *The Sleeping Beauty* ballet with music by Peter Tchaikovsky premiered in St. Petersburg in 1890. In 1959 the animated feature *Sleeping Beauty* was released by Walt Disney and it is considered by some to be his masterpiece.

wasn't invited to the banquet, whose evil spell says the royal child will be pricked by a spindle at age sixteen and die. A good fairy manages to reduce the sentence to a hundred years spent asleep. In an effort to avert this doom, the girl's parents (the king and queen) forbid any spinning, yarn-making, or use of spinning wheels. The princess must be kept from any contact with such things! But when she is sixteen, she climbs a narrow staircase and finds an old woman in a tower, spinning. The foolish princess wants to try this fun-looking activity and gets pricked. As a result she lies in a deathlike sleep (some versions say in a glass coffin) for a hundred years, until a prince finds her and sets her free. They get married and live happily ever after.

Just for fun, let's treat this beloved fairy tale as a modern self-help book. It might be called *Sleeping Beauty, or How to Get the Perfect Man*. Looked at this way, what does it tell us?

- **Number one, avoid spinning.** Don't make yarn. In other words, don't do any productive work. Don't find your own creative path. If you try to, you'll be pricked and doomed.

- **Number two, the best way to end up with your prince is to lie beautifully in a coffin for a century.** Inaction, anyone?

- **The qualifications for getting true love? Nothing too hard.** You need to be a princess. You need to be the most beautiful woman on the earth. In fact, you are *defined* by this beauty: your name is Sleeping Beauty.

- **The man who is right for you has to be a prince.** A perfect, brave, royal man who values you only for your external beauty and your sweet inability to lift a hand in your own cause.

- **You have no say in your own romantic fate.** You made the mistake of trying to create something of your own (spinning), and you have been punished. So you must wait. Your only contribution to what happens is looking nice while you sleep. And your only chance is that the prince, the one who is meant for you and who alone can part the thorny forest that walls in your prison, will come along and find you.

It would be hard to imagine a more perfect metaphor of passivity, or a more perfect insinuation of unworthiness. If true love doesn't find you, it's because you twitched. You should have followed Sleeping Beauty's example, but no. You didn't stay perfectly asleep, your eyelids fluttered. Or if you *did* follow the do-nothing recipe, you must have failed the other big qualification: you weren't the most beautiful in the land. No wonder the right guy never proposed to you.

Now I'm obviously not saying that modern women literally follow this recipe, that they invest in glass coffins and crawl into them with their best makeup on, waiting for a prince. But I am saying that this fairy tale has done some damage. If it had never been told to little girls, big girls would be better off. There is a real attitude in today's world that works against good people finding each other, and that attitude is grounded in, perfectly symbolized by—and even caricatured by—the Sleeping Beauty story. Right down to subtle issues of attractiveness and body type and men caring only about looks; right up to the colossal myth of destiny.

It's all a crock, and it gets in the way of good shopping.

In today's world they invent diseases and mental-health conditions every day—or every time they find a drug solution in search of a problem. So I think it's only fair that we baptize one of our own.

The belief that it is somehow wrong for a woman to play any part in her own romantic fate, and that if she tries to, she will be punished by never getting a mate—let us call this idea and all the thorny myths that encrust it, the Sleeping Beauty Syndrome. Now that we've named it, we can better recognize its creaky voice, laugh it out of the castle, and get on with our shopping, unashamed.

It doesn't hurt that the literary truth is on our side. A little digging reveals that the original story that lies behind "Sleeping Beauty" was a much messier and freer creation. When Giambattista Basile penned the original sleeper tale as part of his *Pentamerone*, published in 1674, the guy who "rescued" the sleeping woman was not in fact her dream man. Before Perrault and Disney prettified the story, the "prince" was not a single prince but a wandering king who was already married to another woman. When he couldn't wake Sleeping Beauty up, he had his way with her in her sleep, and that produced two babies, one of which did eventually awaken the princess by nursing a little too vigorously. Gritty realism, anybody?

But it gets better.

Did Ms. Beauty live happily ever after with her cheating royal?

Decidedly not. First they had to deal with the king's wife, who happened to be an ogre. Understandably enraged at her husband, she tried to eat Sleeping Beauty's babies. That plot was foiled by the cook, who served Queen Casserole with a nice Chianti.

And here my own speculations take over. I would hazard a guess that the real ending goes like this:

> S.B. still wasn't out of the woods. After two years of marriage to the monarch, she could no longer stand his arrogance and divorced him. Exiled from the kingdom by the salacious sovereign, she set up a spinning business in a nearby country. It

took off like gangbusters, and ten years later she fell in love with her accountant and retired rich and happy. Oh, and she kept her own name, which she had changed to Wakeful Beauty.

14

can you be the aggressor?

*Y*ou're making some encounters happen in the real world. You're staying open to everyday opportunities, keeping your antennae on alert when you're in places where you normally go, realizing that you don't have to be *planning* a sighting of a foxy fellow, any more than you have to be planning to see a nice blouse in a store window as you walk down the street. You're also deliberately going to places where you think your kind of man might be, including conversation bars.

You're committed to the unprecedented, groundbreaking Smile Technique, in which a woman smiles at a man because he seems nice and is showing interest in her, thus encouraging him to say something.

But can we take it one step further? Can we make the final break with the Sleeping Beauty Syndrome and say it's okay for you to be the aggressor?

I say we can. I say we must. It's time to step into the twenty-first century and enter the final frontier. We're not just talking the shopping talk. It's time to walk the shopping walk. The few, the proud, the shoppers.

But . . . but . . . there's still this societal voice saying, "Men only fall in love if *they* are the aggressor, and if you are the one who starts the ball rolling, you are forever branded in his mind as pushy, maybe as someone to bed, but not as someone to court."

The simple answer is this: any rule is wrong that lets opportunities go to waste, because there aren't enough opportunities. I say you can be the one who approaches him; you can speak the first line of dialog; *you can even approach a man who hasn't noticed you.* There, I did it—I went too far. What will I propose next, suspending all rules of civilized behavior? What anarchy might result? Am I going to unleash a torrent of heterosexual coupling? To adapt an old Jewish joke, couldn't that lead to dancing? Oh my.

I repeat: in the world that isn't made of pixels, *there are not enough auspicious encounters to let any of them go to waste.* We humans just have to get over this silly social programming and loosen up. We singletons who have not met each other have to realize we are each other's best hope, and stop putting up needless barriers to getting acquainted. Otherwise the females are depending too much on the male side. Otherwise nothing may happen. Even if a desirable guy notices you in the supermarket, he may miss your smile of encouragement or he may not be feeling brave. He may have been taught that it's impolite to approach a "strange" woman and that he could be hauled away as a stalker if he tries. Maybe he just had a fender bender and is a little down on himself. That's why he's breaking his own rules and buying cheddar-horseradish potato chips and olive-imbued salsa.

But the situation is more dire than we've even admitted! You can't always rely on the guy to even *notice* you; he may be having a rare male circuit-failure where he forgets to detect female lusciousness in his vicinity.

But you have noticed him, and the strings of your heart have gone jingle-jangle.

At this point you are the only one who can make something happen. It's you or nobody. Destiny did its part: destiny put you near the strip steak as he was passing the frozen wings. Destiny can do no more.

Now I'll admit this could be difficult if you had to walk up to him and say, "Hi. You look like a nice guy and I was wondering if you would like to join me in a search for true love, marriage, and eventually death." But you don't have to say these things; you don't even have to think them.

And you don't have to proposition him, but by god, you can if you want to.

You can begin more modestly by saying, "I love the smell of this meat cooler." Or, "Planning a big night?" Or, "Have you tried this yogurt? I hear it totally solves IBS."

Even a short conversation, even a little bit of eye contact, is going to reveal a whole lot to each of you, and if interest persists, you should persist too. If you sense real rapport—things have gotten humorous or oddly profound and you've already learned unexpected things about each other and there's been mucho eye contact and you like his scent and he has scoped out your body a couple of times—but he seems too abashed or shocked to muster some kind of offensive that might lead to future interaction—you should step back a pace and say, "I have to get home or I'll never eat tonight." Pause for a beat or two and give him a chance. He will likely make some move toward future contact. If he doesn't and you want to, go for it. Say simply, "Would you like to continue this some other time?" The questioning approach is an excellent tactic, perfected by males all the way back to Socrates. If he says yes, throw him another question: say, "How do we do that?" Challenge his resourcefulness, and his ardor. Make him meet you halfway.

What if some step along this process doesn't bear fruit? Are you hung out to dry? Besmirched forever?

No, you aren't, because you were brave and you tried. There could be a million reasons why he didn't join the party, and most of them are no reflection on you whatsoever.

Whether the outcome is positive or not, all you're guilty of is finding out whether there was an opportunity. And I don't care which degree of aggressiveness you chose. If all you did was encourage a guy who was obviously riveted by you, that's fine. If, at the other extreme, you struck out on your own and awakened a Sleeping Hunk, that's cool too.

In either case or anywhere in between, you have done a service to well-meaning men and women everywhere, to yourself, and to that most excellent fellow who will eventually join hearts with you. Because you know what? In many cases neither person will even remember who started that first conversation, or what it was about. And no fairy's curse has been invoked by you taking the initiative and thus creating a first conversation.

THE BALANCE OF PURSUIT

Now what about down the line: suppose things gel nicely and a series of dates ensues. Can you still be the Valkyrie woman who says, "I make things happen, hear me roar?"

Can you phone him before he phones you? Can you ask him out because a week has passed? Or do we draw the line and admit there's a limit? Do we have to shrink back into the conventional wallpaper and call a halt to female boldness?

I've got a good idea. How about no rules?

How about this: we bear in mind that there should be a *balance* in effort and in risk. So you should avoid creating, or consenting to, a situation where one person is driving the relationship much more than the other. If he is making everything happen and you are just saying yes at regular intervals, that's not good. You need your turn at the wheel too. So, yes, you should be the one calling him and suggesting things, some of the time. Not all the time. We want balance.

Here's why. When one person—let's call them Hare—is consistently the instigator, it can disconnect the other person—Tortoise—from their own feelings. Often this happens because Hare has a quicker romantic pace than Tortoise. Hare is ready to see Tortoise again before Tortoise wants to see Hare. So Tortoise never gets to miss Hare and work up a yearning and think, "I really want Hare in my life and I'm willing to go out on a limb to make that happen."

That's what we humans need in order to develop feelings for each other. After an intense skirmish, we need a chance to assimilate, recharge, and then poke our head out of our shell and make another play. When we're being carried along by someone else's agenda, it's hard for us to tell how far our own feelings are really invested. We need the feeling of our own feet on the ground, pushing us forward.

THE "HEY" THRESHOLD

One area where this balancing act has become extra tricky is, how often do you check in with somebody and say hey and just kind of take their temperature? The cliché is that guys won't call you as often as you want them to. There's some truth to that—with *some* guys. (In Part Five I'll tell you about a guy who definitely *wasn't* guilty of this.)

When two people are out of contact, there's a kind of separation threshold they reach where they need to say "hey" and hear from each other again. What's interesting is that your "hey" thresholds only have to be slightly different to make it seem like there's an ominous pattern. Here's the math. Suppose he would naturally call you every five days but you naturally want to call him every four. So you do. So he never gets to his five-day threshold; he never calls you. So you feel neglected and mistreated. What you need to do is exercise some restraint (and this would equally well apply to him if he is the one with the early dialing finger). Don't call him for a while, and see what happens. In a surprisingly short time he will reach his threshold, feel lonely for you, realize you are worth some initiative, and call you. By doing so he has declared that he notices when there isn't enough *you* in his life. Good. You've restored the balance.

Early in a relationship, when each person is taking perilous steps toward greater involvement, that's what needs to happen. What has made the situation even more tricky in recent years is the advent of texting, Facebook, Twitter, and the rest. There are so many ways of checking in with somebody, some of which don't interrupt what they're doing (supposedly), that one really has to be sensitive on this issue—or be perceived as smothering or nosy or a nuisance—or a hare.[1] Compounding the problem is that you can now monitor whether your new date is online, without doing anything more than logging on to Facebook. In a sense, we are all under surveillance. Post something on somebody's wall and a whole army knows it—friends and maybe their friends and maybe what Facebook modestly calls "everyone."

---

1. Texting is supposedly non-interruptive, but in my experience it is worse than a phone call. A phone call can go to voice mail and you can respond later (or not), but there's something demanding about a text message, and because texting itself is such an inherently clumsy activity, composing a reply can be more distracting than a moment or two on the phone. Not to mention the extra charges many cell phone companies impose.

Again, *viva la balance*. If you are both merrily immersed in mutual messaging, great. But small talk can be tiring, and too much trivial contact can suck the thrill out of a new relationship. More important, if the messaging is one-sided, the perpetrator should get a handle on it and ratchet it down.

Me, I like emails. They take longer to write and, as one friend of mine would say, they are more "thoughty." Emails can be a rich and effective way of getting to know each other better, and if you wait till they reply before you send again, equipoise will be just ducky. In fact, that's not a bad rule of thumb in general: **When in doubt, take turns.** If he contacted you last time, it's now your turn and you get to be the next one to get in touch. And vice versa. Simple but effective.

Summing up: as a relationship develops, both people should share in the instigating and proposing and contacting of one another. You don't have to hang back and be the passive one, but don't do all the doing, either. It's about keeping a balance, and both people need to be aware of it and make adjustments when it gets out of whack. By making adjustments I mean back off when you notice you're doing all the work, and draw the other person out of the bushes. Or if he is pushing too hard, ask *him* to back off so you can feel your wings.

Don't rush him, and don't let him rush you.

A little later (in Part Five) I'll be getting to a very important topic: the trial period you go through with a prospective partner. Those early months are when you decide whether this thing is going to fly or not, and it's much easier to make the right decision if neither person is pushing too hard. In that section I'll talk about the reasons why one person sometimes rushes the other, why the rushee sometimes goes along with it, and how you can set things right. Meanwhile, my point has been that female initiative is not only okay but indispensable, especially when you're trying to make that first meeting happen with a gorgeous galoot. And after you've started seeing each other, you and he both deserve your fair share of the thrill of pursuit.

15

proxy shopping

who is the best matchmaker for you?

Gayle and her friend Talia had been best friends for years. Through major ups and downs, they had always provided a safe haven for each other, always been able to help each other through hurtful times and turn the rest into fun. Talia was exotic looking, mathematical, and a bit of a sorceress. Gayle was a girl-next-door, resourceful and shrewd about people. They didn't seem alike, but their souls meshed perfectly.

They were doing a few errands one day when Gayle said, "You know that antique store on the west side that I'm always telling you about? Let's go there."

Talia saw no reason to say no. They drove over and began to look around, and Talia kept seeing things she liked: a bamboo cane, an ornate umbrella stand, a carved cat. But then she caught her breath and said, "Oh, this. Look at this."

Gayle joined her and they stared at a plaster-cast picture frame, Victorian, cool white, cherubs set in it. It was about ten inches by twelve, with an opening for a small photo.

Talia said, "I can't believe this. This is my dream." She picked it up. "I like these cherubs. They aren't corny. Look how serious the faces are. The wings look strong. Oh no."

There was a "sold" tag hanging from it.

"I'm going to cry," Talia said. "I could die happy if I had this frame. I know exactly what picture I want in it."

"That portrait of your grandmother in the shawl."

"Yes."

"Don't cry."

"I'll never find another like it!"

"You don't have to."

Gayle took it from Talia and carried it over to the proprietor, who was smiling.

"Thanks for holding this for me," Gayle said. "Our plan worked perfectly. She loves it."

She turned to Talia. "Now you can cry," she said, and Talia hugged her.

Sometimes our friends know us as well as we know ourselves, and they go places where we don't go, and they see something they know is perfect for us. That's also true in the realm of mate finding. We need to avail ourselves of their expertise, because it multiplies our odds of finding the one we will cherish.

And, occasionally, they know us *better* than we do.

If you're like me, you can't always be trusted to shop for yourself. If I walk into a Dillard's with the simple goal of purchasing a dress shirt, I can be thrown off my game by the hint of a cross-breeze. If I happen to see myself in a mirror and I'm having a bad face day, I may decide I am too jowly to merit a shirt. If the salesman seems too glamorous, that won't help. If I had a bad day at work, I may doubt my own taste even if I run across the exact shirt that I need, or I may decide it wouldn't fit me anyway, because I've never really found my right neck size and I don't feel like being measured right now. Jeans are even worse. The easy fit is too easy (aka baggy), the snug fit is too snug (unless I stop inhaling), and the straight legs . . . don't exist.

On these bad shopping days, all I manage to do is test my opinion of myself, not the clothes on offer in the store.

That is why I need supervision. I need someone who can make the experience seem hilarious instead of humiliating. And who can spot things that will make me change my pessimist mind.

Something like that is what happened to Suzie with men.

THE GIRL WHO COULDN'T SAY YES

Susie managed a gourmet restaurant in Cincinnati. Her friend Catherine was the chef. Cat was happily married and Suzie, who was not only single but hadn't dated for fifteen years, was their third wheel. Suzie was smart, literate, and dry of wit. Suzie loved fashion—it was her one creative outlet—and she had no trouble shopping for clothes. But oddly enough, that didn't mean she accepted her size-twelve figure, which happened to be a stunning hourglass. She simply was willing to put up with her body in order to decorate it.

Suzie was courted by three men in nine years. Well, not exactly courted, because they couldn't get close enough to do that.

The first man was a wine distributor named Paul. He and Suzie talked a lot on the phone for business and he visited twice a year from California. Suzie told Cat that Paul was the coolest guy she'd ever known, so suave, so knowledgeable. She was obviously sweet on him. On one of his visits, Cat saw them together in the office. Later she drew Suzie aside and said, "This guy is gaga over you. You have to ask him out."

Suzie said, "He doesn't like me."

"He was devouring you with his eyes."

"He wasn't. I'm too fat for him."

One day Suzie reported that Paul had mentioned to her on the phone that he might open an office in Cincinnati.

Cat said, "To which you said . . ."

"Wha'? I said he should talk to Clarence." (A local realtor.)

"You didn't. The correct words would be, 'Let me put together a list of some good locations and I'll take you around.'"

"He doesn't like me that way."

The second man, Boris, was a sous-chef from Georgia—the one next to Russia. He was handsome, smart, hardworking, and had a plan. Cat loved his work in her kitchen. It was clear to her he would own his own restaurant within ten years. And that he had a bad crush on Suzie.

Cat said, "This guy is gaga over you."

"Then why doesn't he ask me out?"

"He's probably afraid to. You're the boss here."

"I'm too intellectual. He doesn't read."

That year when wineman Paul visited, he brought a fiancée and ate some nice pasta made by Boris. Cat pointed out the fiancée to Suzie. "Look at her, she's built just like you. Only larger."

The third man was named Danny. He was an architect, freelancer, and was renovating the back half of the restaurant for the owners. In addition to being a brilliant designer, Danny could quote American poetry and old films. He had read some of the same obscure novels as Suzie.

"This guy is gaga over you," Cat said.

"He isn't. Look at him, he's too young."

"He's seven years younger than you. That doesn't matter. He's smitten."

"How could he be?"

"You're a knockout."

Boris, who was now the chef at a competing establishment, brought his new girlfriend—a professor of English literature—to dinner.

Catherine said, "Damn it, Suze, you are going to listen to me. I talked to Danny. He is crazy about you."

"Well, he did ask to walk me home. Twenty times."

"Tonight you are saying yes."

Suzie said yes. When they got to her place she asked Danny in. She felt he'd earned it: he was boldly venturing where no man had gone. She made martinis and Suzie began to relax.

"I really like you," she said. "Sit beside me."

Danny smiled like a man who has won the slalom. They got married six months later. Catherine, who is also an ordained minister, did the ceremony, as was only right.

If you would trust someone to pick out clothes for you, or antiques, or a good book, you might not want to turn them away when they offer a lead on a good man. I think most of us are our own best matchmakers, but we aren't always in the right mood, and we aren't always there when a good prospect appears. Maybe our friend is.

Some of us are blind to our own strong points. We can't take a compliment, or give one to ourselves. It's hard to blow one's own horn—for many of us it doesn't sit right—but we have no trouble singing the praises of our friends. So a friend may also be able to win you a welcome from a new guy, may recommend you in ways that you wouldn't, may interest him in knowing you for exactly the right reasons. A friend knows what you're capable of. So a friend may be able to talk you into trying someone who takes you out of your comfort zone, into the place where you belong.

The most valuable resource you have is your own awareness, and the most powerful engine for meeting worthy men is you, on your own, in the right place to approach or be approached. But when your own energies are otherwise engaged, it's good to have other shopping eyes on the lookout.

I now turn to the crucial topic of online shopping for love. In Part Four, I present a simple, realistic way to choose the right dating site and find the guy for you on it, and I also describe some specific sites of various types that might be good for you. And I'll explain how to get around the number one problem posed by pay sites. I'm not going to go into all the features of every site, just the ones that matter most.

Onward!

FOUR

SHOPPING FOR MR. RIGHT ONLINE

16

this time it's personals

how your dream man advertised for you

The last thing your dream man does before he crawls into bed at night, and the first thing when he wakes up, is check his email.

Why? To see if there's a letter from you. Or a wink or a nod.

That's because he is looking for you online, and has in fact created advertising meant just for you. Consisting of his excellent face, in a pretty good photo, and some multiple-choice answers about himself and his lifestyle, and a few little essays he wrote, on which he may not have spent enough time, but if he's the right guy for you maybe he did.

Where is this ad of his? It's on a free dating site like PlentyOfFish .com, or a pay site like Match.com or Mate1.com, or a specialty site like SpelunkersNotIntoLadyGaga.com (okay, I made that one up). Or his ad is on a matchmaking site like eHarmony.com or Chemistry .com. Or he could be on a social networking site like Facebook and he's found a way to use it as a dating site (a fascinating option: I'll talk more about it in a moment).

He hopes that you will again *think with him* (collaborate at a distance) and realize he must have done this. He must have created an ad for you to find. So you will sit down in the comfort of your room, sip some Earl Grey, and find it.

He must have done this because, very simply, he'd be a fool not to. To appreciate why, it helps to recall a time before online dating, say the previous century. Back then, you could be lost in the big city, surrounded by thousands and thousands of singletons, knowing there must be a good one for you, but there simply wasn't any good way to prove it. You had to try to meet people on the real byways, and that was much harder. As we've seen, there are ways to optimize that process, but it will never be as easy or as powerful as . . . shopping.

That's right, we have come to a fork in the road, where shopping is not so much a metaphor or a rallying cry, it's simply what you do on a good dating site. What I mean is, *the way you look online for a man is very much the same as the way you would look for a camera or a dress or a book*. Online shopping began with two great pioneers, who invented a new paradigm and got it right: Amazon and eBay. Their gospel spread and now we're all perfectly comfortable with the amazing convenience of looking through a vast inventory, much bigger than any brick-and-mortar store could offer, searching for the exact thing we want, and then ordering it. What impresses me is that online dating not only offers that experience but is in some ways *more* sophisticated than other shopping sites.

Take Match.com. Founded in 1995, Match.com is still one of the biggest and best-designed dating sites, with over 20 million members in twenty-five countries, and with a lavish set of search parameters. If you compare its search engine with the one on the colossal Amazon.com, the dating site doesn't look too shabby. Not only does Match.com allow you to search on more parameters—twenty-six as opposed to two—but it also neatly accommodates the *reciprocal shopping* situation we looked at.[1] You don't need to know which books want you to read them, but you do need to know which men are interested in you, and Match.com has all sorts of ways to make that happen, including winks, call requests, emails, alerts that tell you who has viewed your profile or made you a favorite, and three kinds of matching done by the site (based on the objective info you gave in your profile, not a personality test).

In the real world you don't get to meet many unattached guys, and only *after* you meet them do you learn the basic things about them that would have helped you decide whether they were worth meeting in the first place. Wouldn't it be nice if you could know that stuff *before* meeting them? What a time saver that would be. Well, a dating site can make a good start in that direction by giving you lots of advance info to help you decide which men are worth meeting and getting to know. Plus it lets you choose from a much larger sample of men than you could ever encounter off-line. That is why dating sites get results; that is why hundreds of thousands of people who would otherwise be alone are finding love online.

Think about it. On a good dating site you can search among thousands of men in your area and in the age group you desire, and then can select for such things as appearance, interests, background, values, and lifestyle—before you even look at photos and profiles, let alone make contact. By the time you decide who you might like to meet, you have already accomplished more than you could in a lifetime in the off-line world.

---

1. When you search for a book on Amazon (knowing what you hope to find but not the title or author), you are able to search on keywords (many) and subjects (twenty-nine preset topics). That's only two parameters that relate to content, and both of them may yield so many hits that you get swamped. Once you find a book that is in the ball park, though, Amazon does offer very cool ways of finding similar books.

How do you take advantage of all this power? You need a site that catches the most people in its net, and then most effectively helps you narrow them down. So it must have

1. a lot of active members: the more the better, so you have the biggest sample of men to choose from

2. the best tools to pick out the members who interest *you*

How do you take care of the first point? Well, the sites I've already mentioned are among the top sites in North America, with the most members and the most unique visitors (more significant). But you don't have to take my word for it. On the principle that it's better to be told how to fish than to be given a fish, let me share with you an up-to-date, free resource where you can see current, objective information on the leading dating sites. It's OnlinePersonalsWatch .com. To get rankings, scroll down until the right-hand column shows "Internet Dating Official Rankings," and then choose "U.S. iDating Rankings" or "International Rankings," as you wish. On the Hitwise list for the United States, you will see twenty-five top sites of all types, including free, pay, social networking, and matchmaking sites, and specialized sites for gays, seniors, blacks, and many others. OnlinePersonalsWatch.com was founded in 2004 by brainiac Mark Brooks, and is a cornucopia of news, trends, research, and gossip on every aspect of online dating, including hard business-oriented news.

Okay, what about the second point: which sites allow you to narrow the field down from thousands to a chosen few? This is where search parameters come in. What you want is lots of well-designed parameters—the most you can get for your budget, covering things like age, location, appearance, interests, and lifestyle.

The first thing you do when auditioning a dating site is check out these two points: does it offer enough men in your area (men who look viable to you), and can you effectively select among them? You do this before subscribing (paying), and if a site won't let you see the merchandise before you pay, don't bother with it.

And now we hit a major snag with online dating. (Clearing my throat.) I call it the contact barrier. It is this: some of the members who come up on searches are either off the reservation (no longer paying attention) or haven't paid to be subscribers and so are harder to contact. The latter circumstance applies only to pay sites; the former comes up with free sites too. I will deal with this matter very thoroughly, because it's a serious one. It turns out not to be a deal-breaker.

But let's take things in order.

On to the audition . . .

17

the two searches that reveal
if a dating site is for you

$\mathcal{L}$et's take a free test-drive on Match.com: it's good to experience the Cadillac of dating sites because it'll show you the full spectrum of features. If you have already done some online dating, you will still want to come along for the ride, because I'll be explaining a practical, realistic strategy that can get you past the promises and pitfalls of online dating to the real man you want.

To get into Match.com, you have to be a member (which doesn't mean you have to pay). You'll be prompted to provide an email address, your birthday, and your postal code, but mercifully, not your social security number. And to create a username and password. Go ahead and do these things; that should get you in, though you may also be encouraged to complete your profile. When you're visiting a new site, my advice is don't finish the full profile at this point—just start it; you can come back and do a thoughtful job if you still want to, after you explore the local wildlife.

Time to search. Hit the search button in the navbar at the top. I recommend doing two searches, a catchall and a choosy one.

The catchall search

For the catchall, just do a quick search on men within, say, ten years of your age and thirty miles of your postal code,[1] photos only. Don't limit it in any other way. You should get hundreds or thousands of hits. Choose the gallery view and sort the search results by "Activity date," meaning who has recently visited the site.

Take a gander at the sincere gents on your screen. Go through a couple of pages until you find a cute guy. Pick one who has lots of photos. Okay, now check out his profile. Look at every photo and read the whole thing carefully, including "About Me" and "About My Date." If he got lazy and didn't fill in the details or didn't write a decent intro ("About me and who I'm looking for"), move on and find someone who did. Read *him* instead.

Okay, if you really like this guy and somehow know that he's going to like you, you're done. You've found true love.

For most people, this kind of search can be a bit frustrating. You sit there looking at faces and they start to blur together. You see a face you like and check the profile, and immediately spot three points you don't like:

- The guy seems way too attached to his five dogs.

- His intro is sappy.

- He's looking for women twenty years younger than himself.

You can spend hours doing this on a dating site and lose your sense of direction. There are too many guys, and photos aren't getting you to the right ones.

---

1. Assuming you're in an urban area—otherwise widen the miles or use a nearby urban postal code.

There's a better way, which is the reason dating sites get results. That is to *choose* guys using meaningful criteria, and *then* look at them with an open mind. So it's time to do our choosy search.

The choosy search

On Match.com it's known as a Custom Search. From the Quick Search screen, click on "Keep customizing." Now, in addition to the "BASICS," you'll see twenty-one parameters, each of which can be opened and specified. These are your key to finding more suitable guys.

I'll talk about how exactly to use them in a moment, but first, here's where I'm heading. I'll recommend that you do a smart Custom Search, and when the results come up, you go through them very slowly and look at each man's profile unless his photo absolutely horrifies you. In the real world, people's charm, character, personality, and general worth can transcend or even transform their "looks," but this isn't so true online. When we're looking at photos, paradoxically, we tend to be more superficial, even though photos don't reveal as much. So we need to look deeper. A man who might well appeal to you if you were conversing with him in a café may have a photo that doesn't jump out at you (this may be because he isn't photogenic, or because his photo isn't very good).

But if you have done a careful Custom Search, you have given yourself a reason to give him a chance. Let's see, maybe you asked for men who are your age or ten years older; are within forty miles of you; agree with you on smoking, drinking, and kids; fit you in education, salary range, and political stance; and share some of your most passionate loves in the areas of athletics and leisure pastimes. If a guy fits all this, go easy on his photo and read his essay on himself and his ideal match. Read it carefully. Give him a chance to at least get to the next stage.

You know what you like, and you know when a guy looks and sounds simpatico and sexy to you. But here are a couple of things to watch out for when you read a guy's spiel about himself, or his first emails to you:

- Men who pontificate. Instead of talking to you, he talks at you about what love is or what makes a successful relationship. He's lecturing on his exalted views. He may do the same thing for thirty years if you hook up with him.

- Men who define the woman they want in overly reverential terms, turning her into an angel on a pedestal. A variation on this is the guy who lists his requirements for his woman in ominous words like: "The young lady to whom I will give my love will be bright, earnest, compassionate, fetching, loyal, giving, and never cantankerous." (Sounds more like a dog, doesn't it?) This can signal one of two things: he is old-fashioned in his views on women and actually wants to be your boss (whom you serve); or he is a perfectionist who will forever be trying to find fault with you. Or both.

- Men who seem to fall in love without the niceties of meeting you and getting to know you—before you've even spoken on the phone. Mr. Over-Eager is probably needy, desperate, attached, or lives with his mother. If he can fall in love so easily he doesn't really care who it's with, so he is prone to shallow attachments that peter out as fast as they form.

Another thing to be careful of online, odd as it may sound, is mistaking attention for compatibility. If we don't get a lot of responses on a site, we may overreact when someone does show interest. "False positives" are part of the allure of the online arena. When it's suddenly more possible to meet a potential date than it was on the mean streets, that can lead to the illusion of things being good, when they are really just stimulating. So don't let "he's interested" become equivalent to "he's the one for me." If he's knocking on your screen, that's good news (especially if your ad is honest and complete—see below), but it doesn't mean he's the right one; it means you have to *find out* if he's the right one.

As I said a moment ago, however, **the biggest pitfall of DIY online dating is not that we may give someone too much credence; it is that we may overlook a gem, by reverting to a more shallow attitude and letting a person's photo stop us from going where real passion waits.**[2]

That said, it's time to look more closely at the tools that can get us past this snare.

---

2. By DIY online dating I mean the sites where you can search and browse for yourself, as opposed to sites like eHarmony where you surrender the matchmaking to the site.

18

how to do a custom search
for your custom man

There are a couple of crucial things to know about search parameters. They are not hard to grasp, and if you aren't aware of them, you may cut yourself off from the very guy you're looking for. The angel is in the details. Somewhere.

Some parameters are useful to know *after* you locate a good profile, but you may not want to stipulate them in your search. For example:

- eye color

- hair color

- occupation

Once you find a great guy, it's nice to know his eye color; but it would be a pity to miss your dream dude, who is perfect for you in all other ways, because you specified blue eyes in your search and his are hazel. Similarly with occupation; can you really predict which occupations qualify a man to have his profile seen by you? What if a guy is everything you want and his job doesn't reflect his soul, or maybe he is soon to change careers to one you approve of?

What might surprise you about occupation and what makes some parameters especially tricky is that it is a *single-choice* parameter. That is a crucial thing to notice. It means that when your dream man creates his profile, he is confined to one answer.

This contrasts with a category like "sports and exercise" where he can click as many choices as he wants.[1]

Obviously eye color and hair color deserve to be single-choice; most people have only one of each (though exceptions immediately come to mind). But not so fast with occupation. Match.com offers twenty types of job (plus "other" and "no answer"), but a person must choose only one when creating their profile. What if the man you seek has three things he does for a living? Or what if his occupation doesn't fit any of the presets so he chooses one that's only approximate, or checks "other" or "no answer"? The *search* screen lets you include more than one choice; for example, you might specify legal, sales, and educational. But if you aren't inclusive enough, you may still miss the one he chose, even if you would actually like what he does for a living. (If he chose "no answer," you have to do that too or you'll exclude him.) So if you want to specify occupation in your search, check off as many as you can, and consider doing another search sometime where you leave occupation open (choose "no answer").

The general rule: **On the search end, be as inclusive as you can when he had only one choice in his profile.**

---

1. To understand this, go to Profile on the navbar and choose Edit Profile, then explore. You'll find that some parameters allow you to tick more than one choice and some don't. As I discuss various sites, I'll mention single-choice parameters that could trip you up.

Religion is another fiddly one. A member profile can only hold one of Match.com's twelve choices. If you definitely want your man to be a Christian Catholic, go for it, but remember that this is a topic with lots of gray areas. Some people don't feel comfortable in cookie-cutter slots. A man may have a lot of trouble choosing between atheist, agnostic, and "spiritual but not religious," the last of which really means, "I have reservations about organized religion but I also value what I call sacred, and have unanswered questions and yearnings about the cosmos and my soul," or something like that. Many people who were raised in a traditional religion may choose that designation. So don't confine your search to a very few choices unless you're really sure; and don't casually omit a choice just because you don't like the wording. He may have chosen it reluctantly. Even if you are a fervent believer and want a man who shares that, don't exclude any choices that might qualify. A man may be a serious Christian but not subscribe to either Catholicism or Protestantism. (Match lets him say "Christian-other.")[2]

Finally, there's body type. It may be good to search on, depending on how important it is to you, and it is informative *after* you come across an interesting guy. Match.com breaks the male body down into six types: slender, athletic and toned, about average, a few extra pounds, stocky, and heavyset. (Unlike many sites, they graciously avoided more derogatory wordings. This makes it more likely that people will be honest.) You can search for as many body types as you want. If you're a guy searching for a woman, you get those six, plus three more: curvy, full-figured, and big-and-beautiful. But this is still a single-choicer: when creating a profile, only one option is allowed. You may think you are both slender and curvy, but Match.com makes you say you're one or the other. A guy may think he is

---

2. Be advised that all five DIY dating sites I'll be discussing have religion as a single-choice parameter.

stocky *and* athletic, but he has no way of telling you this. Marie may not want to call herself "full-figured" (many women think it sounds matronly), so she chooses "curvy." But Tim, who loves bodies like Marie's, may search on full-figured and thus miss Marie. Same with slender. The word may put you off, but the lean lion who was forced to choose it may not (he wasn't offered "lean"). Therefore be as accurate as you can when describing yourself, and when you're searching, only exclude things that you absolutely can't abide.

How about *multi-choice parameters* like sports and exercise and common interests? They are more forgiving. Mr. Right got to check as many choices as he wanted in his profile, so you have a better chance that your selections (in your search) will hit pay dirt. So relax with them.

Within a given parameter, you get more hits by ticking off more items. But it's still true that the more parameters you call for in your search, the *fewer* hits you're going to get. That's all very fine and dandy if you notice that you've narrowed the thousands down to a cozy little group that includes some cool guys. But if they don't show up, you may want to widen the distance from your postal code, say, to fifty or a hundred miles. If you still don't get enough hits to be meaningful, clear some of the parameters you chose or widen the radius or the age range even more. (I'll talk later about whether to widen the search to long distance, and tell you my own story.)

Rainy-day searches

Another fun pastime on a rainy Saturday is to pick one parameter that interests you, say education or common interests or occupation, and just explore it, as an experiment. Meaning loosen up on everything else, just to see who's out there! Don't specify any other parameter (except maybe location), and just see who comes up. Your fantasy for the day might be guys who are into camping, cooking, and travel. So tick those under Common Interests and make sure all other parameters are not engaged. Maybe you'll find someone who appeals to you muchly, even though he's not in exactly the age range you usually designate . . . And maybe you'll discover he's looking for you.

Keyword searches

Another option deserving of the "playful experiment" approach is the keyword search. When you want to see guys who used a certain word in any of their essay answers (say arugula or Harley or coral), try searching on it. Match.com profiles also include self-chosen MatchWords to enlarge the keyword universe. A word of caution here: a keyword search will succeed only when the guy you seek happens to have used the exact word you type in. This can be a very powerful feature when it works, but it can also exclude lots of viable guys. Don't add it to every search you do, but do give it a whirl when you're in the mood to explore. A search like this, based on two keywords, led my spouse to me, so I know it sometimes has far-reaching results.

Okay, you've done two main searches, the catchall and the choosy; you've experimented with parameters. If you found some men who really interest you, and their description of who they're looking for sounds like you, then you know this site is a contender. You can either continue your tour of well-attended sites (more on that below), or you can take the leap and subscribe (pay), which will give you the ability to email members and read emails from them.[3] If you do subscribe, you'll also want to go back to your profile and finish filling it in.

---

3. On Match.com as of this writing, this will cost you $34.99 for one month, or less per month for longer packages. Beware of free trials and six-month guarantees, on Match.com or any other site. The free trials require you to opt out before the trial ends and are easy to blow; the guarantees have small print stating what efforts you have to make during the six months and you may fail to qualify. It's better to spring for one month or if you are flush with funds, go for a package of more months and save money. In either case, find a way to remind yourself to cancel if you don't want to continue, so you won't be rebilled.

But what if you haven't found any suitable swains. Should you give up on Match.com?

Not quite yet.

You should still finish creating the best profile you can and accessorize it with a good set of photos. Here's why—and how.

19

the best shoppers advertise too

One good reason to make your own online ad as complete and as "you" as possible is that if you respond to a guy's ad, the first thing he'll do is check out your profile and photos. That will be his first take on you, and may be the deciding one.

The second reason is that your dream man may be out there, and he may have an ad, but you may still not find him. Yet if you have a good ad, he may find you. Why is this so?

Well, you may miss his ad completely, for one of the reasons we've already touched on:

- He filled in some parameter with an answer that you excluded in your search. He said he was "agnostic" and you searched on "spiritual but not religious." But it turns out that you are very similar and compatible in your religious thoughts.

- He is outside the mileage range or the age range of your search. But if you met him and got to know him, you would want to be with him anyway. (More on the long-distance issue later.)

Or maybe you *did* see his ad but you didn't bite. That could be because his face isn't the kind to jump out at you, though if you met him you would be delighted by how he looks. (Some people just don't come through in photos.) Or it could be because his essay on himself isn't exactly to your taste.

But maybe he does spot your ad, because he formulates a wider search and gets more hits, and takes the time to go through them and come across you. And as luck would have it, you do jump out at him as a terrific person that he wants to meet. Perhaps you have a face that *does* have that instant appeal (at least to him), or you found a charming, funny way to describe yourself that lets him know you are his type. The fact is, not all people are good at formulating introductions to themselves. It's a form of advertising, and advertising is a talent like any other. Many folks find it especially hard to sell themselves, not realizing there are ways around this (you can do a soft sell based more on charm, quirks, and humor than on "how great I am").

Because searching is not an exact science, and because not everyone succeeds in coming across in a personal ad, it's better for you and your eventual mate to both have ads out there.

To optimize your ad, I'll begin with some tips on your photos:

- **Don't use a photo that shows you at a different weight or a different age—like ten (or twenty) years ago.** I know some people do this, but humanity's collective truth score goes up for every one who doesn't. Don't be outside in the sun squinting, or shaded by a big-brimmed hat. Take those sunglasses off. Don't include pics of yourself with what looks like your loving partner. If you just have to use a photo that was taken with your ex, maybe you can Photoshop him out of it, but try not to leave a phantom hand on your shoulder!

- **Get a good photo.** Don't use whatever you have lying around; this is too important. Don't even think about not posting a photo: some sites won't let you do that, and all of them say correctly that you have a *much* higher chance of your ad being looked at if you have photos on it. If you don't have a good pic, ask a talented friend to take some shots of you. Someone with a good eye. Avoid some professional portrait photographers who tend to make people look like stuffed animals sitting in front of phony clouds. If you have a great smile, use it; but moody is good too if you look irresistible that way. Anything is good if it expresses the real you and is not much less, or much more, gorgeous than you really are. Remember this: the more misleading your photo is, the more likely it is that when you first meet a guy, he won't react to you the way he reacted to your ad. Since the point is to meet people in person, misleading ads are only sowing the seeds of disappointment and embarrassment.

- **Post several photos.** You need at least one good face shot, and at least one good full-length shot in clothes that don't conceal your shape. Best is a set of photos, four or more, that have some fun in them. Avoid what I've seen a lot of: filling out your photo set with five portraits that are just variations on the same shot at the same time. We want different perspectives on you, different moments, lightings, angles.

- **If the dating site you're on allows videos, by all means do a short one.** (Most laptops have built-in cameras these days, or you can do a short flick using your digital camera.) *Plan what you're going to say or even script it.* A video conveys you in a much more dimensional way, if you take a little trouble over it. Avoid common video mistakes: I've seen a snippet of a vague figure running through the woods, a faltering speech that says, "I guess you've read my profile and are looking at my video now," a video that introduces the person's dogs instead of the person, a video where nothing happens, and a nice shot of someone not looking at the camera. Do what many people apparently don't: watch your video after you make it and see if you like it! Make your video playful and fun; it's more important to convey that than any facts or demands.

Now to the rest of your ad. We've already gone over issues about parameters; choose carefully when you're filling in single-choicers. If several descriptions apply to you, try to imagine what your ideal guy would search on. And be accurate.

That leaves the essay questions—chances for you to express yourself in your own words.[1] These little prose forays are to online dating what your personality is to a live encounter: absolutely crucial. Especially the big one, your main intro to who you are and who you're looking for. My best advice is to express your original, divine, witty, quirky, lovely self, showing a capacity to enjoy life and some substance too. Above all, *concentrate on things that are unique about you.* Here are some tips:

- **Don't say things that everyone would say.** Don't say "I want a caring, honest, two-way relationship with humor and sensuality, close yet independent, and by the way, you have to be my honest-to-god soulmate." These are laudable goals, but the

---

1. Match.com gives people ten chances to write their own ad copy, plus a headline. The main one describes yourself and your ideal match (up to nine hundred words); the others are fifty-word snippets on favorite things, ethnicity, faith, job, and pets.

trouble is everyone agrees on them. These stipulations and fifty cents won't get you a Chai Grande—not the lipstick or the tea. They are generic and cliché. A man may accept them all and have nothing else in common with you.

- **Don't start on a rant that is really a portrait of the cad you were stuck with last time.** In this category are statements about how you're looking for an honest man, a guy who won't cheat on you, a guy who isn't mean or abusive, and so on. What these words convey is that you were burned last time. They could make you come off as bitter or angry, and unfortunately they tend to attract the very guys whom you're trying to avoid. That's because dishonest dudes sense easy pickin's.

- **When you're looking for a new man, start with a clean slate; turn the page.** You need to believe that there are good men out there and you're going to find one, and approach your next lover with an open heart, not with suspicion or paranoia. You need to have gotten over that past relationship that haunted you, and learned its lessons, or you will live in a state of rebound, forging a weird threesome where your new man has to share you with the ghost of your old man.[2] All of us have baggage but we need to be able to carry it, not be buried under it. It's good, eventually, to share with your new soulmate the journey you've taken, the times you got your heart broken, and the things you learned. But don't share these things before you've met and made friends.

---

2. I wrote a book about this. It's called *Better Love Next Time* and it might as easily have been called *What Your Broken Heart Is Trying to Tell You or How to Heal Your Romantic Soul*. It talks about the ways in which we are not whole after a failed relationship, and what we can do not only to recover but to understand what we really want, next time around.

- **Imagine the guy you want and talk to him.** Don't worry about the rest. Instead of trying to appeal to all men, talk about specific positive things that you know some men won't relate to, but the right guy will. For example, what kind of TV shows you like *and don't like*. What sports bother you, which ones you enjoy. What music you like, and don't. Causes you believe in. Political stances you reject. Things and people you value. Favorite couple activities. What you would dream of doing with him on a vacation. What food you like to eat, and what you like to cook. And any other window on your world and on what gives you joy. Always be specific; nail the detail because that's where the flavor is.

- **Don't give out your locator info (last name, workplace, phone number, address) till you have met the guy and feel sure of him.** (This raises a huge issue about Facebook as a dating instrument, which I'll discuss in Chapter 22.)

20
the contact barrier

$\mathcal{I}$n an ideal world, all the members you see when you do a search would be 100 percent available for communication, should you find them interesting. But unfortunately that isn't true. Let's see why.

Both pay and free sites suffer from what we may call *absentees*—people who gave up, moved on, or found someone, and maybe aren't even receiving notifications from the site (or aren't paying attention to them). They're still members, but at the moment they aren't interested. So they really don't count. They're like people in the real world who aren't looking. You can't blame dating sites for them still being onboard, but they are a misleading presence. They are essentially unreachable.

In addition to this, pay sites have a special problem: members who *are* active but haven't forked over the money to subscribe, so they don't have the same ability to communicate that subscribers have. On Match.com these people can't initiate an email to another member or open one sent to them by a subscriber. (I mean internal Match.com emails that protect the "real" email address.) In fact, they can't even see who it is who sent the email to them. They just get a notice that they've received an email.[1]

What *can* non-subscribers do? They can send a wink, or reply to a wink they've received. Winkees can see who winked at them. Doesn't sound like much . . .

The argument against pay sites

Some people say this all adds up to a fatal flaw in pay sites. Let's run a typical scenario. Suppose you are reconnoitering Match.com and you see a fascinating fellow. You are trying to decide whether this site merits your money. What if the guy is an absentee? You better test him. So you wink at him.

And he doesn't wink back. Problem: you can't tell if he is an absentee who never saw your wink or if he actually looked at your profile and wasn't interested enough to wink back. Now what if he *does* wink back at you? Well, now you know he's paying attention and he likes you enough to muster a wink—that's promising. So you wait for an email from him—oops, you won't know if he emails you unless you subscribe. Your in-box may say there are emails for you, but you don't know who sent them.

Okay, when this happens a few times—a return wink from a cool-seeming man—should you bite the bullet and subscribe? (After all, it's only $35.) Let's say you do. Then you send him an eloquent email. And you don't get an email back. Shucks, now you don't know if he read it and passed on you, or if he isn't a subscriber and didn't even

---

1. Just how big is the non-subscriber problem? Based on the 2010 Q1 report for its parent company IAC, Match has 1.6 million subscribers. It also has claimed 20 million members. (These numbers are not well defined and may include other dating sites grouped as part of Match, and more territories than North America.) Anyway, it is likely that the ratio is no better than one in twelve. On the other hand, *active* members are more likely to be subscribers, so the ratio of subscribers among men you actually look at is probably healthier.

know it was you who had sent it, let alone what was in it.

There are many variations on this scenario, but you get the point. There's a kind of barrier caused by absentees and non-subscribers. And no easy way to jump over it.

What is a shopper to do? Should she stay clear of pay sites like Match? Are they futile compared to a free site like PlentyOfFish?

My answer is no.

The solution to the contact barrier

Your job as a shopper is to get to a decision on any guy who interests you, as to whether he's worth pursuing. And you can still do that, even in the situation Match presents. Here's how.

You can avoid wasting time on absentees by sorting your search results as I recommended, on activity date—how recently the person was on the site. That way, most of the guys you're looking at are paying attention.[2] (And probably a higher proportion of them are subscribers.) Match also shows you how recently each person has been online, up to three weeks.

Now, if you wink at one of these active joes, he will check out your info. If he is a subscriber, he can send you a brilliant email and start the wheels turning. And here's the pivotal point:

If he isn't a subscriber and your excellent profile and photos aren't enough to make him pay $35 to know you better, even though you winked at him, then *he isn't the guy you're looking for.*

---

2. If your chosen guy is simply not active, then he wasn't available to you anyway, so you've done all you can. And free sites have many non-active members too, so they aren't superior in this regard. All of the DIY sites I discuss let you sort by recent online activity, except Zoosk, where it may be the default.

So you've handily eliminated him; you've reached that decision, which is all you need. Move on and look for the right guy.

Which only goes to show how absolutely important it is that you have a really good profile and photos, good enough that you are fine with losing any joes who aren't galvanized by them.

Oh—one thing. You need to subscribe so you can receive emails from these gung-ho guys who care enough about you to pay up, and from the noble ones who have already paid their dues.

So there is still a leap of faith, but it's not that bad. Reconnoiter the site before you pay. If interesting men wink at you or return your wink, chances are some of them are already subscribers or will subscribe to meet you. So take the plunge. If none of them works out, you may well find others who do, and at the worst you've only lost a little pocket change and you reached a decision point on some interesting men.

A final twist: if you pay an extra three dollars per month when subscribing to Match, and subscribe for three months, you can have a feature called Email Read Notification, which tells you if and when any Match email you send is read by your intended recipient. That is nice because when you send an email to a guy, you can tell the difference between getting no response because he never read it (probably because he's non-active or a non-subscriber) versus no response though he did read it. If this kind of closure is important to you, you can get it.

I've used Match as an illustration because it has well-developed parameters and also is a good example of the contact barrier. I'm not saying it's the best pay site—that call is up to you. As I continue this tour, I will describe three more pay sites: Mate1, Lavalife, and Zoosk. I'll note where each of them sits regarding the non-subscriber problem (it turns out that the first two offer an easier path than Match, while Zoosk doesn't). I'll also be describing the free site PlentyOfFish and the matchmaking site eHarmony.

A final note: as you probably realized, there's a good reason why pay sites are resistant to letting non-subscribers send or receive emails or IMs (instant messages). They don't want you to be able to give or receive information that would allow you to meet someone without paying. Because then they'd miss a major part of their revenue. They allow you to exchange winks because winks don't give you a way of connecting with the other person.

What is more puzzling is why Match won't even tell you *who* emailed you. Wouldn't that give you an incentive to subscribe? I pondered this and made the following guess: Match must have done a study to determine which is more likely to make you pay—an email from someone who isn't identified (so you can't check their profile) or an email from someone who is. They must have found that mystery is more appealing than knowledge—in other words, that seeing who emailed you is less likely to make you subscribe than not seeing. As usual, fantasy is more powerful than reality.

21

other sites, other prices

Okay, we've had a test-drive in the Cadillac of pay dating sites—what about the rest?

First, it's worth noting that if there's a smaller niche you want to be in, there's probably a site for it. If you want to search within your ethnic group, age range, or any other category, just Google "dating site for ____" and you'll find lots of options. Go for the most heavily trafficked site that fits your bill. (Due to space constraints I'll stay with more general sites in my survey.)

PAY SITES

Besides Match.com, two others deserve special notice here.

Mate1

In Canada or the United States, Mate1.com is of special interest because although it's a pay site for men, at this writing *it is free for women to use*. Men have to subscribe to see all of your photos, send or read emails/IMs, or see who's viewed their profile, but these things are free for women.[1] Thus you get one of the main advantages of a pay site, which is that the men on it have to be serious enough to pay a monthly fee if they want to meet you; yet you get the budgetary benefit of paying nothing. You never have to make that leap of faith as to whether to subscribe, because you're already in.

So you can use the strategy I've explained, and it won't cost you a dime. When you find an interesting guy, send a "flirt" (like a wink). Send an email too if you like. If he's interested and is a subscriber, you're already past the barrier. If he hasn't paid yet, he may decide to—in which case you're again good to pursue it. If he decides not to subscribe, that is your answer.

Note that on Mate1, when a guy sends you a flirt, it looks to you like a short email, but it's actually boilerplate language offered by the site. You'll quickly learn which wordings are not true emails; don't assume that the guy is a subscriber until you get a real email or IM.

Also worth noting about Mate1 is that it doubles as an adult site. This is because its profile and its advanced search include a section called Sexual Preference, and that can be used to send a hooking-up signal.

Notable single-choice parameters are occupation, body type, religion, and the six lifestyle parameters, so be inclusive when searching on them.

Shopper's tip: Do not ignore the keyword search on Mate1. It is the only way to search on Occupation, Field of Study, Favorite Things, Least Favorite Things, and some of the entries under body type, plus (as is more usual) the self-penned essays About Myself and

---

1. At this writing, Mate1 costs men $49.99 for one month, and less per month for longer packages.

Who I'm Looking For.[2] On Mate1 the keyword search is not part of the main search, but it does allow you to narrow the field in various ways.[3] Favorite Things deserves mention as a cool profile section that helps define an individual: it gives the user forty directed blanks to fill in for items such as comedian, travel destination, indulgence, and leisure activity; and the very useful Least Favorite Things gives you twelve juicy categories to rant about.

Lavalife.com

Especially if you're in Canada, where it has more impressive rankings, Lavalife.com merits a look; it is refreshingly different in its layout, is quick and easy to navigate, offers many convenient searches, includes member videos, and has departments for Dating, Relationship, and Intimate. That means you can have three distinct profiles, but that isn't as much work as it sounds. When you create a profile for Dating or Relationship, Lavalife clones it for the other. If you want, you can also fill in three "Since You Asked" entries for Dating or three "Have in Common" entries for Relationship. Lavalife has a layout of Interests that can only be called lavish, with a huge selection of multiple-choice options under

- Outdoor Activities/Fitness

- Entertainment

---

2. That's because there are discrepancies between Mate1's profile-creating screen and its search screen: some multiple-choice wordings are different between the two, and some multiple-choice profile options are not on the search screen but can be accessed through the keyword search.

3. You can narrow the initial keyword search by gender, age range, photos only, and "online now." The first results screen can be further refined by body type, distance, and ethnicity.

- Hobbies and Other Interests

- Sports (Participate and/or Watch)

All these can be single-checked or double-checked, so they're effectively *ranked*.

An excellent feature of Lavalife is that you can put your photos in your own Backstage area, where a member can only see them if you choose to send him a "backstage pass." This means that you can be discreet, protecting your more personal or private pictures from exposure and reserving them for those who win your confidence. (It also allows people to reveal their identity only to those they choose— which could make things easier for cheating spouses.)

What about the contact barrier? Lavalife offers its own chink in the wall, amazingly, by allowing anyone to *reply* for free to emails and IMs from subscribers. So if a guy sends you an email/IM, you can read it and see who he is, and without subscribing you can email/IM him back (and if things go well, eventually meet him). What you can't do without paying is message guys who haven't first contacted you. But you *can* send them a "smile," which may get the ball rolling if they have paid up. So you have lots of options: you can get all the way to meeting men without subscribing; or if you decide to subscribe, guys who haven't paid can respond to you, or send you a smile and maybe get you to contact them. So the barrier is still there, but it's only half as high. For the real fun to begin, at some point one of the two people has to subscribe, but it doesn't necessarily have to be you.[4]

---

4. At this writing, Lavalife costs C$34.99 for one month, less per month for longer packages.

On Lavalife the recently online feature is a search parameter in the advanced search. You can search for those "online now" or who have been online in the past seven, thirty, or ninety days. So you know you're looking at live wires.

About videos: my quick survey indicates that many men on Lavalife don't have videos, and those who have don't always work too hard on them, but some are expressive and even the bad ones can be plenty revealing.

FREE SITES

On free sites everyone gets all the privileges for none of the money.[5] You'll notice a plainer interface and commercial ads (that's what brings in the revenues), but ads are now found on pay sites too. If you find the guy you're looking for, you have literally lost nothing.

PlentyOfFish.com

PlentyOfFish.com is the king here. It has been around since 2003, is huge in membership (at or near the top for visitors, including pay sites), and now even has a free personality test that takes about five minutes and claims to predict whom you're most likely to date or marry.[6] Photos may look slightly distorted. The search engine is not as sophisticated as a site like Match.com, but it ain't bad (twenty parameters, not as well worked out). The Interests category is a single blank filled in manually by users and searchable through a keyword

---

5. I'm talking here about sites that are free for men as well as for women. Mate1, as I said, straddles the two categories of paid and free, offering women the advantage of a pay site without the cost.

6. In March 2010, PlentyOfFish beat all others for average daily visitors. See http://plentyoffish .wordpress.com/2010/04/28/match-com-no-longer-top-dating-site-sends-in-the-lawyers/ for a blog about this.

search, so it's harder to predict which subjects they may have covered. Words in people's self-penned intro are not searchable. The editorial tone of the site is a bit blunt.

You can sort by Last Visit on advanced search. Search results tell you when someone was online, up to thirty days.

To boost revenues, in 2009 PlentyOfFish added the option of a paid upgrade to "Serious Member," a tone-deaf choice of terms suggesting that all non-paying members are *not* serious, but let's overlook that. To win the privilege of paying, you have to pass a quiz purporting to reveal whether you're capable of a long-term relationship. If you pass, then for a small fee (starting at $9.80 a month for three months) you can upgrade to seriosity, and this is predicted to net you more emails, a gold-colored listing, and other boons.

Some people think that a free site doesn't attract the same quality of members, especially regarding desire for a long-term relationship, but given the sheer numbers of people on PlentyOfFish, there have to be some who are looking for lasting love. And you can select for that: one of the parameters is what the user is looking for, including Long-Term, Dating, Friendship, Hang Out, and Intimate Encounter.[7] Again, you can find out for free if your type of guy is on the site.

MATCHMAKING SITES

Many sites have the ability to match you with other members, based on objective parameters (e.g., Match.com) or on personality tests (e.g., PlentyOfFish). These sites also allow you to be your own matchmaker, by searching and browsing members and seeing who you can

---

7. You can select more than one choice within this parameter by holding down shift or control. This is also true of profession, education, body type, and income.

find and who you like. But a few sites want the matchmaking all to themselves and don't allow you to search or browse their membership on your own. The most ambitious (and currently the most expensive) of these is eHarmony.com.[8]

eHarmony.com

The eHarmony site puts you through a massive personality test that may take you an hour, or maybe more if you find questions perplexing when you don't know their purpose. After that, they issue you a personality profile and then their mysterious matching mechanism kicks into gear. It uses the results of their test to figure out which members are right for each other based on eHarmony's proprietary twenty-nine dimensions of compatibility. You can't look through their millions of members and find your own matches. You *can* see your test profile without paying, and you can see some of your matches (though not their photos).

Whether eHarmony is for you has a lot to do with how you feel about personality tests. If you believe that scientists can take an accurate reading on your psyche by asking you questions many of which are vague, lacking in context, and cryptic in purpose, you're off to a good start. If you also believe that these people who haven't met you can then predict which men's profiles go with yours—in other words, which men you are going to find attractive, get along with, and eventually want a serious relationship with (and have all these feelings returned), you are off to the races.

Some people actually want an inscrutable agency to select their partner for them. Of course, they still have to choose among the

---

8. As of this writing, eHarmony costs $59.95 for one month, and less per month for longer packages.

matches that eHarmony comes up with, but they *like* the air of mystery surrounding this lineup of people. The very fact that they don't know how the prospects were chosen somehow makes the situation more romantic, more cosmic, and more persuasive. So Dr. Neil Clark Warren's algorithm becomes the modern version of destiny. *If I choose my true love, he could be wrong for me, 'cause I'm fallible. But if Destiny chose him, I'm home free!* There's a self-fulfilling aspect to this logic, kind of like a placebo effect. Bathed in the certainty that eHarmony has the magic formula for matching, a couple may "find" a cure for their loneliness in each other, the way consumers of placebos in antidepressant trials often find relief from the blues.[9]

But I say it all comes down to proxy shopping. You have to decide who you trust to do your shopping for you. I've said that friends or family who know you well and have met the guy in question can sometimes steer you right. It's a matter of whether you believe scientists have advanced far enough to quantify your romantic soul, and thousands of men's, without having met any of you.

When you don't have time to shop and if you do put stock in personality tests, eHarmony has the virtue that it does the work for you. It may also cause you to look beyond appearances, because after paying the substantial fee, you are likely to consider each match even if his photo doesn't drive you wild with desire. And you may find men who don't rate appearance as so important.

If you're interested in eHarmony, I suggest you take their test and scrutinize the profile in which they describe you and the kind of man you're suited to. Then look at some matches (to the extent you can without a photo) and see if they sound good. If you feel that all

---

9. Studies in 1998 and 2010 showed, in fact, that antidepressant placebos are only slightly less beneficial than real antidepressant pills. Visit http://www.newsweek.com/2010/01/28/the-depressing-news-about-antidepressants.html for the *Newsweek* report.

these things are spot on, you may have a reason to take the next step and subscribe.

And that leaves social networking, and in particular, Facebook. Is it good for dating? Let's see.

22

can Facebook get you to Mr. Right?

(and the Zoosk story)

$\mathcal{F}$acebook has conquered the world. It is such a huge phenomenon, with such staggering membership figures, that one can't help wondering what it could do as a dating site. At half a billion members worldwide, its unique visitors dwarf those of the top dating sites by a factor of twenty-five or more.[1] It's become part of the daily life of many people, who have invested time and loving care in decorating their Facebook pages with personal information, photos, links, status comments, responses to others' posts, things they "like," and a host of other valued objects.

Now what if you could sit down at your Facebook screen and use it as a dating site?

What would be good about that? Well, the window that Facebook provides on a person is often more personal and candid than what you find on a typical dating site. They aren't trying to hide their everyday self, aren't trying to impress you or persuade you to want them. Perusing a person's profile on Facebook is more like being

---

1. See U.S. numbers on OnlinePersonalsWatch.com.

invited into their home, where you look around at their furniture and photos and plants and pets while they make you a cup of tea. But it goes beyond that. You get to see what kind of people their friends and family are, and in their own posts you get a running commentary on their daily life.

So you think, "If I could just find the Facebook members in my area who are unattached and looking, and the right gender, and the right age range, and maybe the ones who have an education level that I would want . . ." and you realize what you are dreaming of is that Facebook would have a search engine like a typical dating site. And you could search on all members, not just your friends or their friends. And instead of friending a person you could date-friend them, and they would look at your profile and respond . . .

That's what it would take. But as soon as you think about it, you realize that Facebook doesn't have anything like this kind of search ability. It could, but it doesn't. (I took a look at the Info screen in Facebook's Profile and was surprised to find that Facebook has already nailed down at least fourteen dating-relevant parameters, plus bio and favorite quotations.)

You can search for people by name, and you can search for words that come up in people's posts. You can search on a word like "Toronto" and get all the posts that mention Toronto or even an unstructured list of all the Facebook members in Toronto, but that's a bit intimidating even for a browsing champion. You can't even begin to do the kind of search that any good dating site would afford you.

Why is that? It's because Facebook's special philosophy has been to enable people to communicate with their own friends, near and far, recent and long past, family and not. Its purpose was primarily to connect you more richly with people you do know, not people you don't know. And to allow you to share your life with this controlled network. Which grows by extending bonds through friends to their friends, and so on.

It is true that there has been a titanic internal struggle between Facebook's original spirit and its commercial desire to get you to share more and more of yourself with what it calls "everyone"—so that advertisers would pay to target its huge, diverse, self-defined demographic populations. Privacy controls—and our own privacy settings—were revised without a lot of fanfare, so we would wake up and find that non-friends and even non–Facebook members could see more of our info than we'd ever bargained for. Then an outcry, then revised privacy controls—as the beast stumbled and learned to walk again on more complicated terrain, with a lot of members barely aware of the problem.

So the issue was up for grabs and the golden plum still dangled from the tree: what if Facebook (with its gazillions of members in all their warm, personalized glory) could be harnessed to a dating engine?

Then came Zoosk.

In 2007, some clever guys with a lot of start-up money gave a Christmas present to the world: they started plastering a dating application all over social networking sites like Facebook, MySpace, and Bebo, offering to make dating fun again by letting people find dates within the context of social media. Their strategy paid off in burgeoning membership: by 2010 Zoosk had risen to the top five of all dating sites in the United States and Canada.

So, did they make our dream come true? Is Facebook now a dating site?

Well, not exactly.

What Zoosk did was to get a lot of social network users to join Zoosk. In other words, it quickly became a dating site with a lot of members.[2] We like that. But how good a dating site is it? Seen on its own, Zoosk is a serviceable site, but it is not nearly as well developed as the top dating sites (more in a moment). What about its association with Facebook—does that somehow make it excel?

Put another way, does Zoosk somehow lay open the whole Facebook world to the dating impulse; does it break the privacy bonds of Facebook, allowing you the kind of access to all Facebook members that you now have to your Facebook friends?

Well, sort of. A lot of Facebook members joined Zoosk—millions of them. So if you search on Zoosk you'll often find one of them, and if you get interested, you are now hip to a Facebook member who wants to date. But can you see their Facebook profile? That depends on how they respond if you friend them. On Facebook.

And therein lies the rub.

Because the fact remains, a lot of us didn't intend our Facebook info to go to just anyone.[3] I wouldn't have put so much of my personal self into my Facebook profile if I intended the world to see it. Would you? Privacy is important. Suppose a guy contacts you on Zoosk and is interested. So you exchange a couple of emails and you're thinking about meeting him. Do you friend him on Facebook? Consider this:

- Do you want to show him all your personal photos? Is it time for that yet? (Even the ones where you got tagged while cavorting after five martinis?)

---

2. Zoosk claims over 50 million at this writing. See its Help page under "Why should I become a premium member?"

3. As Facebook so awkwardly puts it when you encounter the profile of someone who isn't one of your friends, so-and-so "only shares some of his profile information with everyone." The first time I read this, I thought, well if he only shares it with *everyone,* I'd hate to see what he does when he's feeling more reckless . . .

- Do you want to give him access to all your friends? Facebook can make an orgy of friending happen in a very short time—that's what makes it so attractive. But is that what you normally do with new dates?

- Do you want your dialogs with him to take place in front of your friends? When he playfully posts on your wall (or you on his), that's what will happen. But friends draw conclusions so quickly, and escalate things, and gossip, and interfere . . .

- Do you want your dialogs with your friends to take place in front of him? Are you ready for that?

- What if things get intense and then something goes wrong and now he's out to get you? Sure, you can unfriend him, but what about all your friends—will they remember to, or will he be able to paper their walls with his feelings?

After all, there's a process where we slowly introduce new lovers to our world, to ourselves, and to our friends and relatives. Zoosk hasn't given us a reason to change that. In fact, in its own coaching on how to fill in the "About You" section of its profile, Zoosk urges you not to provide email, Facebook, or MySpace IDs, or other identifiable information. Don't even give out your Facebook name, let alone friend someone on Facebook. (This advice, of course, benefits Zoosk financially, because two people don't need Zoosk once they are friends on Facebook.)

Another irony is that Zoosk claims to target primarily people under age thirty (65 percent of its members).[4] But compared with older

---

4. And 24 percent of its members are aged thirty to thirty-nine. See Zoosk fact sheet at http://www.zoosk.com/press.php?from=footer for this statement.

users, people under thirty are exactly those who, according to a recent Pew Survey, "are not only the most attentive to customizing their privacy settings and limiting what they share via their profiles, but . . . are also generally less trusting of the sites that host their content." The survey goes on to say that "Social networking users are especially attuned to the intricacies of online reputation management. Two-thirds now say that they have changed the privacy settings for their profile to restrict what they share with others online."[5] So the very people whom Zoosk targets are the most likely to hesitate to give someone a window on their Facebook world.

Still, Zoosk has a boatload of members who spend a lot of time online and are young. So if that's your demographic, you'll want to check it out. Here are some points to bear in mind:

- Zoosk can help you fill in your profile by migrating certain information from your Facebook profile, including your photo, which they may do even if you haven't installed a photo on Zoosk. (This happens if you installed Zoosk as an application on a social network like Facebook.)

- If you find someone on any other dating site, he also has a good chance of being on Facebook, and one of you can ask to be Facebook friends if you want to. You probably have as good (or bad) a chance of getting a yes as you would if you met through Zoosk. So it really comes back to number of members.

---

5. Pew Internet and American Life Project on Managing Your Online Profile, May 26, 2010, http://pewresearch.org/pubs/1606/managing-your-online-reputation-profile-facebook-searching-for-ourselves.

- If you join Zoosk as an application on Facebook, some of your delicious flirting activities on Zoosk will show up on your wall on Facebook. You can turn this off if you wish or you can join Zoosk directly on www.Zoosk.com—that way, according to Zoosk, your activities won't get on Facebook's news feed.

- Zoosk's situation regarding the contact barrier is much like Match's. You can exchange winks without paying. But when you try to open an email, you find that the conversation has been "locked"—and can only be unlocked by subscribing.[6] You can't read or respond to an email unless you pay. You can, however, see who emailed you (unlike on Match). Zoosk says that premium membership will get you "unrestricted ability to contact . . . singles across the Zoosk network," along with advantageous placement of your profile in search results.[7] Those who read the "unrestricted" claim might be surprised to know that many of their email recipients can't open the emails.

- Compared to other major pay sites, Zoosk can only be called slapdash. For a site that claims such a huge membership, it doesn't provide impressive tools for narrowing them down, lacking many of the parameters found on other sites. There is no keyword search. There are no sort options for search results, and the display only tells you if people are "recently online" or not; the word "recently" is not defined. (It's possible the default sort is

---

6. "To unlock conversations, non-premium members must purchase a premium subscription." Visit http://answers.yahoo.com/question/index?qid=20100429094043AAEKBm5 to find this quotation from the Zoosk support team.

7. See Zoosk Help page under "Why should I become a premium member?" at http://www.zoosk.com/help.php?from=top-right for these statements. At this writing, Zoosk premium membership costs $29.95 for one month, less per month for longer packages.

by how recently a member has been online.) The "Basics" in the profile are all single-choice; the rest aren't searchable.

- If you want to see which of your Facebook friends are using the Zoosk application, at this writing you can go to http://www.facebook.com/zooskdating and see their names and pictures. How long this will remain true, I am not sure. If you want to gather some interesting data (and think they won't mind), ask your friends if they have subscribed to Zoosk, or ever used it.

The bottom line here: Zoosk caught on like wildfire, because it appealed to millions of wannabe daters on Facebook and MySpace. At 50 million, Zoosk's membership is now a tenth as big as Facebook's, which is saying a lot. We don't know yet whether Zoosk will turn out to be the greatest thing since . . . Facebook, or a fad. We don't know how many premium members it has, and we don't know how many people joined Zoosk and then lost interest. So we don't know if it's going to be the dominant dating site of the decade or not.

But there's a chance it will, and it certainly has beaucoup members, so it's worth a try.

23

what about long-distance love?

my own story

$\mathcal{I}$ said in Chapter 18 that you may miss your dream person because he is outside the mileage range you specified in your online search. That could mean you chose a fifty-mile range and he is fifty-two miles away. You can get around that problem by sometimes searching on a wider range. But what about people in another state or another country?

I've heard quite a few stories about couples who met online when they lived far away from each other, and one of the two eventually relocated, and they are doing great. Such tales might give you pause. If people want love badly enough, they'll cross any gap to get it. And sometimes you just can't find it nearby.

One of these stories I didn't hear—I lived it.

My spouse and I met online when we lived 850 miles apart, and it was four months before we met in person, during which time we got to know each other very well by email and by talking for hours on the phone. We had much in common, including similar feelings about our childhoods, which for both of us had involved a beloved summer place. We were very interested in each other, craved in-person contact, and exchanged all the photos we could find, including snapshots from childhood. We became close friends without having met. In some ways that made it easier to spill our guts to each other—our fears, dreams, and hopes, and our war stories about love.

Then came the day when I flew to Philly to meet her. We were terrified because what if we didn't have chemistry, what if the vibe wasn't right? It would have been incredibly awkward to have to abandon the "history" we already had, which we (foolishly—don't try this at home) had allowed to take on a romantic flavor. I had met other women online, and a couple of them had been in other cities, but things had never gotten so far and when it didn't click, it was okay, a pleasant visit that simply didn't gel into something more.

But this was different: we had a lot to lose.

When we first set eyes on each other she was wearing a jaunty black beret with white polka dots, so I could identify her. She smiled at me and for the first time I saw who she was—her photos had confused me, because she has the kind of face that looks different every time you see it. But at least this was the real her I was looking at, and that helped a lot. I liked her face and I loved the winsome "isn't this nutty" look in her eyes. My nervousness made me think I needed a coffee (not really the antidote), so we bought one on the way to Baggage Claim. Then, as the suitcases crawled by, I kissed her. That went well, we seemed to know what to do.

For me, the next few days were a strange ride, a roller coaster. Sometimes she seemed like the person I had known at a distance, and sometimes she seemed a complete stranger. Nature gets confused when you get so far ahead of what it calls real, and wants the meter reset to zero when you physically meet. We crossed to New Jersey and slept in her parents' house while they were away. We camped in the rain and could barely light a fire. We went to an old hotel on the coast where I met everyone she worked with and was reviewed by some very daunting women whom she called the "Board of Doubts." I had culture shock and person shock. We started to know each other as real people. We weren't as facile in person as we'd been on the phone. We weren't as good at listening—there was too much distracting us. We were sometimes in very sweet territory, but it was unknown territory. One day in a restaurant she was explaining what the Christmas holidays could mean and I had a sudden stab of love for her. I went for a walk alone and knew that hopes I had almost abandoned were alive again. I sat under a tree and my world was changing around me, and it brought me to tears.

Then I was on a train to the airport and my feelings reversed themselves two or three times as I tried to add it all up and be sure of something. Finally I settled into a contentment and paged through every image from our time together as the tracks clicked beneath me.

We went through more visits in the next year and we nearly broke up several times—because it's hard enough joining two people who are not kids anymore; but it's really hard when you have separate lives and are trying to bond during the brief intermissions. But eventually we knew we had to try it. She moved to be with me in Nashville seven months of the year (she was able to telecommute), and the other five she worked at the old hotel in Jersey. During those months apart we would fall back on our original phone-only relationship and get close in a different way, which seemed to patch up our fault lines. (Later, the situation flipped for us: she got a year-round job she couldn't leave and I was now self-employed and could go to her.) There are no guarantees, but so far it has worked out pretty well for us.

But this was supposed to be about online searches. I was glad she had not limited her search to her own area; but then, she lived in a place where there are not huge numbers of unattached straight males, and she was feeling feisty the night she typed some words and found me. I think she was just fantasizing about a soulmate, and kind of daring the universe to ante up—"I'm here, I'm ready; whatcha got, life—who's out there for me?"

I don't tell this story to recommend the long-distance thing (it's definitely a big risk). But I can't speak against it either, and when you think about it, it isn't as outlandish as it might seem. These days, a lot of people are pretty flexible as to where they might live; their location is somewhat of an accident. It obviously helps if one of the two can telecommute, as happened for us. Or if one partner works for a corporation or chain that has offices in many cities. Also, some folks have friends or family scattered around a large region such as the northeast, and so could settle into any of several urban centers.

If you cast your net to the wider world in search of a soulmate, try very hard to avoid these two pitfalls:

1. building up too much passion at a distance and then having it fizzle on first meeting

2. not taking enough time to know each other (a proper trial period) before one of you relocates to join the other, and then discovering it isn't going to work

Scenario one is awkward and painful and hard to sort out honestly until you are back to the phone or email. It will do less damage if you are both aware that it could happen and give each other permission to feel however you feel. Scenario two is even tougher, but again, if you both acknowledge the possibility, you buys your ticket and you takes your chances. Breakups are always possible during the trial period, and some good may still come of such a story: a new city, new friends, new opportunities may open up for the one who moved.

All that said, it's still best to start in your own region, especially if you live in a large urban area. But if you don't find Mr. Right there, that doesn't mean the excursion is over.

24
from virtual to real

$\mathcal{A}$fter you've been in the online dating world for a while, it can seem incredible when you set up a real meeting with a real person. So when that day comes, there's a tendency to load it up with too many expectations.

But just as you interacted online with lots of men who didn't turn out to be worth pursuing, you're going to meet some guys in person with whom there is no fit. Sometimes that will be because he isn't interested. Sometimes you. It's disappointing, but don't let yourself get discouraged and give up. Keep your eye on the prize and stay with it.

When you and a promising guy have emailed and/or talked on the phone, *as soon as you both know you're really interested, meet in person.* Don't dilly dally for weeks or months in the virtual world, possibly getting ahead of yourselves emotionally. Take advantage of the fact that you aren't a thousand miles apart, and meet face to face. That is the only way to see what's happening. And keep these tips in mind for that meeting:

- **Try to take a Zen attitude so you aren't too nervous or appre-hensive.** Don't have an agenda, other than to *gain information.* Treat the meeting as a test of the potential couple, not of you personally. If you don't warm to him, he isn't the dude for you. If he doesn't warm to you, he isn't the dude for you. Information gained. And done.

- **Don't agree to a romantic dinner or a whole evening with someone you haven't met.** Make it coffee or a drink, and that way you can exit gracefully, if needed. On the other hand, if things are going like gangbusters, you can always decide to extend the visit.

- **Follow safety guidelines that are posted on good dating sites.** Choose a quiet public place where it's easy to talk.

- **If the conversation lags or stumbles, ask him about himself.** That will get most men talking. Then note how long it takes him to ask about you. If he never does, it may be because he's too adrenalized to think of that. Or maybe he's not the good conver-sationalist you're looking for.

- **Even if things go well, cool your love jets for a while.** Don't assume, based only on the first meeting, that he is gung ho and attracted. Some men, in an effort to put their best foot forward, will turn on the charm and act like they are seized with enthusi-asm. Some men just can't deliver bad news to the one whom it affects. I'm not saying don't be optimistic if things seem to have gone well; I'm saying hedge your bets, hang on to your heart, and wait for further confirmation. If he really is smitten, it will come quickly.

The best possible outcome is that you get along as people *and* you are attracted to each other. If so, you will very likely agree to meet again. That's a wonderful feeling, worth celebrating, and there's a chance it may lead to a lifelong relationship. But it may not. That's why it marks the beginning of the most important stage of all in shopping for Mr. Right.

The trial period: when you get to know each other and see if the two of you were made for this. It's my subject in the next section.

FIVE

THE TRIAL PERIOD—AND BEYOND

25

testing love by trying love

*O*kay, you have reached a milestone on the road to love. By hook or by crook, by a good effort online or off, you've made things happen. And during your latest encounter with a guy, sparks flew. Eyes lit up, smiles gleamed, conversation flowed.

He wants to see you again.

Is your shopping done?

No, it's just getting started.

You can figure out whether you like a dress by seeing it in a store and wearing it once or twice. But in the case of a new guy, one or two meetings or a few dates won't even scratch the surface of what you need to know about each other. Not hardly. It takes months to get an idea whether you have enough in common to go for it as a couple.

Some chemistry and a nice conversation are great signs. But you don't know enough yet. You need a trial period, a "getting to know each other" time, during which you don't make an irrevocable commitment, because you realize that this person may not turn out to be the one. How long should it take? Well, it can end at any time if it becomes clear that things aren't going to work out. But if things keep progressing and passing new hurdles, I think the trial period can last as long as six months or more.

But what do most of us do once there's a definite sense of romantic interest? We start acting like couples. We spend a lot of time in each other's company, doing a sort of audition of monogamy, being affectionate, keeping in touch, making plans, starting to extend the circle to friends and family, acting in many ways like we've been together for years. Yet we aren't really "together"; we haven't made a commitment, we may not be ready to say "I love you." It's what we call *seeing someone,* a sort of attachment-that-isn't-attachment.

And here's the weirdest part: we aren't wrong. Because *the only way to test love is to try love.* So we get this experiment where two people try on the role of "true lovers" to see if it fits. It's kind of like playacting in good faith, a "fake it till you make it" foray. But it's a tricky process, because we don't always remember that it's just a test, and when one person decides to jump ship, the other can be confused, hurt, and angry. Still, fair is fair. There has to be a way to find out if two people belong together, and if the verdict is no, that has to be okay too. No harm, no foul.

The alternative approach is to studiously "keep it casual," taking small steps and not moving to new levels unless you're sure. Unfortunately it doesn't work, because it never lets the trial period happen. Too much caution means people get stuck in a platonic pattern and can't find a way out. If you don't join hands or kiss when the impulse is new, you may never do it; and if you're afraid to act like a couple, you may never become one. You don't get to be sure in advance: you have to blunder ahead and see how it feels.

So I vote for the first approach, testing love by trying it, with these suggestions:

- **Both people should be clear that you're just trying the relationship out.** If either person wants to end it at some point, that's okay.

- **Bear in mind that it's the combination of you and him that is being tested, not you as an individual or him as an individual.** That is how you protect yourself from being hurt—you don't take the outcome too personally.

- **Neither person gets to sweep the other along, or rush them.** In Chapter 14, "Can you be the aggressor?" I talked about how both people deserve a turn at the wheel. I'll pick up the thread in Chapter 28. It's an important factor in the trial period.

- **When little escalations occur (like the first time somebody says "I love you"—okay, that's huge), they have to be seen as trial balloons.** So if he's the one who takes that risky step, that means you can't hold him to it—not yet, and it also means he has to notice if he's made you uncomfortable. It's almost like there are two tracks, one where you two are "in the role," trying new things on for size, and a more objective one where you keep an eye on what commitments have actually been made.

- **Don't jump the gun.** At the start, there's a tendency to go off half-cocked. Feeling the rush of having found someone who is attractive, nice to be with, and available, people jump the gun. It's not that they immediately fall in love, it's more that they get overexcited about the new plan and treat it as a fait accompli. I've had emails from readers who report that they've found the one, after two dates. It's sort of like a "get rich quick" frenzy, where someone hears about a new investment and puts all their money on it without a closer look. As I read their letters, I can tell they are betting all their chips based on no evidence at all, just a good conversation and a kiss; they don't even know the person yet. My answer: cool your jets and test it out, and if your feeling is confirmed by the evidence, that'll only make things better. If it isn't confirmed, then you've saved yourself a huge disappointment.

- **Don't go to sleep at the wheel and forget that this is a trial period.** It's all too easy to drift onward for months or years, forgetting that you were supposed to be figuring out if this guy was the one, and failing to take notice of the red flags that mean he isn't. It takes guts to admit it isn't working out and it takes energy to get back in the game and try again; but that's what separates the shopper from the also-rans. So keep your wits about you, take stock at regular intervals, and if it isn't working, face it.

- **Don't return him before you've given him a chance.** Because the window for returning a new purchase can be so short, we sometimes panic and take it back before we really got to try it out. This can apply in spades with a guy you've just met, so it's important to remember that you have lots of time to explore and you *will* have a chance to say no if you want to. Realize that the right person sometimes takes some getting used to, especially if you've been accustomed to being with the wrong guys. It's like those makeover shows where the subject has to be led kicking and crying to the strange new wardrobe that she will eventually realize brings out the best in her. (I'm talking about the episodes where they don't divest her of her natural identity.)

- **Use your time wisely and conduct a thorough vetting of the couple.**[1] Don't shy away from trying things or asking questions because you fear that the answers may be negative. They may very well be positive.

Successful people welcome deal-breakers. That last bullet point deserves expanding, because it is the very essence of the shopping spirit. Passive people get mired in poor situations because they are too afraid of bad news to probe the truth. It is a mark of successful people that they are able to eliminate bad options efficiently because they put them to the test. It's just like with shopping. When you're in a store and you see a cool item, you check the label, ask questions, try it on—confronting the possibility that it won't be your dream come true. If you find out it doesn't fit right, there's no return policy, it's going to shrink, or the fabric doesn't breathe, you walk away and you're better off.

Every time you say, "No, this isn't it," you get one step closer to what you want and refine your sense of it. You benefit.

I talked in Chapter 14 about how it's okay to be the aggressor and try talking to an interesting man, because you get an answer, instead of wondering for the rest of your life whether he (and countless others like him) might have been worth knowing. That point applies even more when you're starting to see a guy and you need to know, is he the one? You should feel free to check out every aspect of him that matters to you, *even if you might uncover a deal-breaker.* "I don't want to do anything to upset the developing relationship" is

---

1. Vetting is of course what governments do when an important appointment is in the offing, what employers do when a promising applicant appears, and what the rest of us do when somebody's bona fides need examining. In this case it means taking a close look at a new man and relationship—putting them through their paces to see if they are what you wish.

a bad rationale! "I'm afraid to try x because it might reveal that we are wrong for each other" is the ostrich approach. You can't find Mr. Right if you never realize that the one you're dating is Mr. Wrong.

That's why, in the next chapter, I'll give you a proactive game plan that will help you and your new man show your true colors to each other.

26

your own love lab

*G*ood fortune comes to those who are willing to take risks and test their dream. So it's time to find out what you and Mr. Possible have got. Here are twelve exciting diversions that will help focus the trial period and make it productive.

During the first six months to a year, try to complete at least seven of the following items, preferably more. (Many of them may happen naturally; a few are diabolically designed to take you out of your comfort zone.) If you don't get through seven of them in six months, that's fine—you just need a longer trial period. Like baseball, love is not a timed game: it takes as long as it takes.[1] The right moment to commit is when you've learned enough about each other, not when you've logged *x* months together.

If any of these assignments scare you, make them mandatory.

Here they are:

---

1. This is one of the fascinating things about "America's pastime." Most professional sports are subject to a rigid timer and consume a definite duration (other than overtime); baseball just whiles away nine innings.

1. Go on a road trip to a place neither of you have been before, for at least three days—just the two of you. Take turns driving, map-reading, and so on. If possible, get lost at least once.

2. Whichever of you is less versed in cooking, make a meal for the other.

3. Visit his parents (and yours) and stay overnight if you can. If parents aren't doable, visit another close family member. Try for a dinner with a wider group. If convenient, talk to some of his family members without him present.

4. Throw a party and both invite your best friends, so they get a chance to mingle.

5. Each of you tell the other about a major challenge you've faced at work, how you handled it, and what the outcome was. (This should happen more than once.)

6. Spend a night together where the goal is not necessarily intercourse, and where he learns (you teach him) a good way to make you summon the deity, if he doesn't already know. And vice versa, by all means.

7. Spend a day together with no screens—no computers, cell phones, TVs, or movies. Also no forms of passive entertainment, like watching other people play a sport. Real books are allowed, if one of you reads to the other. Talk, walk, go on outings, stay home, explore, whatever, actively enjoy the day.

8. Go shopping together. Make two excursions, one where he helps you with your mission, one where you help him. Examples: shop for a car, for home furnishings or décor, for clothing. Pick the products you think will be most revealing of your psyches.

9. Have a friendly debate about matters that you disagree on. (You'll find suggested topics at the end of this chapter.)

10. Attend the wedding of one of his/your friends and keep your ears open.

11. Make four lists. (Do this by the six-month point.)

   The first two lists you do on your own, then read to each other:
   • Three things you've learned from the other person

   • Your top three goals for the next ten years

   The next two lists you formulate together:
   • Three movies/books you both adore, with reasons why

   • Three people you know whom you rate as human beings (poor, okay, good, or excellent), where you try to agree on the rating. If you can't agree, talk about why; if you can, share your reasons for each rating.

12. Sit down together and have an honest discussion about your respective finances. This may come near the end of the test run, maybe when you're thinking of moving in together or getting engaged.

Assessment

Every few months, or whenever you feel like it, it's good to step back from the relationship and assess how it is going. I've designed the activities in the above list to help that process, by generating meaty data for you to ponder.

To spark ideas as you think about the state of the potential union, here are questions you can pose to yourself. (Some relate particularly to the twelve activities, some don't.)

- Are you able to share the lead when you do things together? Or does one person take over? If one person is less skilled at a certain activity, are they forced to back off and concede the ground?

- When a plan goes off the rails and things aren't perfectly under control, how do you each react? Are you able to have fun with it? Are you able to improvise as a team?

- Are you a team?

- Are you able to entertain each other, or do you exit into separate worlds (screens, gadgets) when you're alone together?

- Does he listen to you; and when he does, do you feel as if he is the person you *want* listening to you?

- Do you feel like yourself with him, or do you feel you're being dragged away from your own real identity? Does he intensify your dreams, hopes, and loves, or does he seem to dilute them?

- How do you feel when he's there with your friends and family? It's kind of like the first time you wear a new dress for your peeps. Do you feel fabulous? Do you feel more like yourself, or less? Does his presence enrich the experience of being with them, or does it suppress the connection?

- Is he able to take an interest in things you do, even if they don't directly concern him and especially if he doesn't know a lot about them? Can you do the same for him? This will emerge especially in the shopping activity. Do you like his taste, his choices, his opinions of yours?

- Do you like what he chooses to spend money on, and how much he spends? Does he seem to think of the two of you as people who might one day share financial assets? Do you? If either of you have financial problems, do you think you could tackle them together? Can you trust him with money? (There is no shame—not these days—in having financial troubles. The only shame is not to face them.)

And here are a few more factors to look for, which call for a bit more expansion.

Complementing each other

It helps for couples to be alike in certain ways, such as values, desire for children, intellect, energy, sexual agenda, and humor; but in other areas, like life skills, they may thrive on not resembling each other. It's nice if each person brings different strengths to the table. But to truly complement each other, they have to get off on each other's gifts. For example, maybe one member of the couple is more of a people person and can effortlessly connect with boatloads of folks and even remember their relatives' names and histories. Whereas the other member of the couple doesn't have that chip in such abundance. Then the question is all about attitude. Does the less social one delight in what the other brings, or resent gifts that he lacks, so it becomes a problem and creates a wall?

Emotional openness

An important ingredient to look for in a long-term partner is that the emotional lines of communication are open, they're just naturally open with that person. You're able to be unguarded with each other, able to comfort each other, express sadness and hurt to each other, and simple joy too. (As the years go by, the unselfish urges to nurture, protect, and support the other person will find a fertile base in this soil.)

With some people you find yourself being clever in a coldish way, you feel like your ego's more in play (which can still allow friendship). But in a partner, that can create a wall. When you try to be open, you feel as if the other person is seeing you as corny or maudlin—so you default to acting cool. Partners need on occasion to be uncool, to be as a child with each other.

The Carfax report

How do you peer into a person's future? One good way is to look at their past. When you're buying a used car, you can look at a handy thing called the Carfax report. Based on a VIN (vehicle identification number) check, it tells you how many owners the car has had, whether it's been in serious accidents or floods, whether it has frame damage, and so on.

Can you get the Carfax report on your new beau? Yes, you can. His family and friends constitute a rich source of information about where he's been and who he is now. They know him best. Not only that, but they are a reflection on him, and your feelings about them should heavily influence your take on him.

I'm not saying this in a simplistic way. I'm not saying, if you don't like his family then you shouldn't like him. Many parents are far from perfect, and many of us have hang-ups and conflicts around our parents, and a mixture of love and resentment. And un-resolved issues that we deal with as best we can, even after they're gone. Many parents are pretty terrific (even heroic in what obstacles they've overcome) and some even provide a template of what a good marriage is.

So it's not whether his parents are "great" (though it's wonderful if you like them), it's whether you can understand how he feels about them and treats them, and understand *him* better having met *them*. Do you like who he is when he's with them? Do you see him carrying on their attitudes or habits, for good or ill?

What else can you learn from his family? Well, it's good to know in advance why the whole thing's going to go south, if it is doomed. So go to that wedding where his relatives are gathered (or that extended family dinner), and listen to the drunkest, most cynical person at the event—maybe some leathery old aunt. Check out what she has to say about his family and about him. Because that'll give you the worst-case picture. You don't have to believe her, but at least you'll know the argument for the prosecution.

With friends it's a bit simpler. We don't choose our families, but we do choose our friends. So the question is, do you like his choices? Or do you feel he has built booby traps into his life by surrounding himself with defective, unreliable people? Do you want his friends as your own? My rating exercise comes in here, where you and your guy rate three people you know and try to reach agreement.

Much depends on whether you and he can see eye to eye on the people who walk through your life.

If you have children in future, some of them will be more like you and some more like him. Kind of like your respective friends. If your judgments of these people are at odds now, that could be a preview of whether you will see eye to eye on your children, and *their* friends. There are no guarantees in love, but one of the best assets a couple can have is that they are in sync about the characters who star in their world. And if you each enlarge the other's circle, that is a true blessing.

When looking at his past, you can't ignore his past relationships, or his exes. You may not get to talk to any of these women, but if you do, you may learn a lot. Equally revealing is how he talks about them. Look for rueful admissions from him, among the critical remarks. Does he give himself a fair share of the blame? Look for understanding, and a desire to do better. Is he one of those gladder and wiser people I talked about in Chapter 7? That would be good.

Another potent source of information about your new guy is Google. Take a deep breath before trying this. Search on his screennames as well as his real name. Check out videos and images too. Have fun! You may dig up nothing harmful, or you may find he is currently married for the fourth time, was quoted in a local paper as supporting the Ku Klux Klan, or is being sought by the FBI under another name.

Finally, reprising some early topics:

- **Ego:** How does his opinion of himself compare to his actual merit and accomplishments—as you see both? If it's too inflated, that's a bad sign. If it's too low, maybe he just needs validation—but how badly, and are you prepared to give it? Another angle: how wrapped up, or embroiled, is he in the question of his own worth—does he constantly worry about it? Does his self-esteem seem to be on a roller coaster? Sustaining it could be a full-time job for a partner.

- **Testosterone:** First, does he have enough? *This is a very subjective thing.* A guy who seems effete to one woman may seem perfectly masculine to another. Take your own reading, over time, and trust it. Second, do you like where his testosterone is channeled? As I said in Chapter 1, most men have certain issues where they won't back down—the things that arouse the sleeping lion in them, where they will go to the wall. Do his choices sit well with you? Do you like where his backbone lies? It may take a while to tease this out, but there will come a day when you see him rise ardently to the defense of something—a friend, a football team, a principle, a stranger who's being abused, his family, his country, you . . . Take note of what he fights for. Third, watch how he reacts to victory and defeat—I mean everyday wins and losses. Some people revel in aggression and competitiveness. They like to turn every situation into a zero-sum game; they'll wager you about when the roses are going to bloom. This too is a matter of personal taste: so check it out in him and yourself.

- **Dimensions of affinity:** In Chapter 10, I discussed six kinds of magnetism that pull two people toward each other. They were sex and desire, admiration, interest, respect, and that sly dog, entertainment. (He *is* a sly dog, because he doesn't care whether people are nice or noble, just whether they make the time fly.)

When you step back and assess your relationship, run the six dimensions through your mind and see how they're holding up. Do you feel each of them for your guy? Are they deepening over time? Do you feel them coming back to you from him?

In the short term, these things will fluctuate. Some days you'll worship him, some days he'll worship you. Some days you can't believe someone so interesting would seek your thoughts. Some days he is afraid of you. That's all fine, but when you take a longer view, if things have slipped way out of kilter, then Houston has a problem. If one person is looking up a steep hill at the other, feels the cold air of indifference, that's no good. When people are well matched, mutual regard is self-correcting. They both just naturally do things that jerk the other person to attention and make them feel awe. Or ah. Or aw . . .

The early months of a relationship are thrilling, challenging, scary, delicious, and crucial to knowing if you should commit. The whole trial period raises unique questions, many of which I've been asked by readers:

- If you fall in love, does that prove you're with the right guy?

- Why do people sometimes rush the relationship even when they've agreed not to? Does this indicate a deeper problem, and can it be solved?

- Why does a guy suddenly disappear when things were going so well? Is it commitment-phobia or something else?

- Should you judge a man by what he is now, or by what he could be?

- If you have fights, does that mean it's not going to work out?

I'll answer them in the next few chapters.

Topics for debate

Activity number 9 is to have a friendly debate about some matters that you disagree on, to get at beliefs and values that you live by.

I suggest that you sit down with your guy and spitball some topics. Take a first look at each topic and see if there seems to be agreement. If so, keep looking. When you sense difference of opinion or non-comprehension of either person's point of view, that's gold. Add the topic to your list and find at least three.

Here are topics to consider, but I encourage you to think up your own based on what you know of each other:

- Is it good to share fears and worries with your partner?

- What makes a man manly and a woman womanly? (Any answer is okay, including "nothing," but the point is to discuss if you disagree.) How rigid is your code of each?

- Which is more important, your job or the things it makes possible?

- Politics: find a burning issue of the day that you don't agree on or have trouble understanding.

- Religion: if it's important to either of you, don't leave this topic out. Possible questions are whether it should be taught to children and whether a certain organized religion is "right" and all others wrong.

- Do you agree with same-sex marriage?

- Which countries would you like to travel to, and what do you think you can learn from other cultures?

- If you have children, will your relationship with them be more important than your relationship with each other?

When you discuss your chosen subjects, stay calm and cool, don't yell, and give each person time to finish their thought before the other replies. The purpose of the exercise is not to see who wins or who's right: it's to see where there are fault lines, whether you can deal with them amicably, and how you feel about each other with this new data.

27

if you fall in love, does that prove you're with the right guy?

(The Love Hoax)

One of the jobs of a shopper's guide is to talk about scams that are in the air that can make people buy bad products—faulty, deceptive, and in this case, heartbreaking.

What makes a phony product especially hard to resist is if you haven't had too many looks at the alternative: the genuine article. It's hard to shop for something if you have no model of what you're seeking. And that is totally true of relationships. We see so many ailing marriages in real life, and so many train-wreck couples on TV, that it's hard to remember what a good relationship even looks like. Maybe your parents had one, but maybe they didn't. Then along comes the great sham, promoted by a giant ad campaign . . .

The Love Hoax.

It's a major bill of goods that is being sold every day.[1] And it's the biggest enemy of deep, lasting, fulfilling, *real* love. It's the myth of

---

1. It's being pitched by movies, TV, and other media, and used to sell weddings, gowns, jewelry, chocolates, roses, travel, makeovers, hotel rooms, cars, credit cards, shampoo, clothing, music, laundry detergent, and alcohol. It goes back a long way: some say to the eleventh-century troubadours of Courtly Love; some say fairy tales like "Sleeping Beauty", "Snow White", and "Cinderella"; and some say Darwin wired it into our brains long, long ago.

Perfect Eternal Bliss, which couples buy into and try to live up to. It's a hoax, perpetrated on innocent people, and it leads you astray and robs you of what you could have. If you want to know why so many shoppers don't find Mr. Right, or don't end up happy with him, *this is the reason.*

Call it Cupid's big scam.[2] It's the idea that destiny leads you to a perfect soulmate and then you marry them and the two of you have bliss forever after, basting in adoration and mind-boggling sex.

How does Cupid close the sale on this myth? He puts you into an altered state that we humans refer to as "falling madly in love." That state is so powerful that it catapults you right out of reality and into a fairy tale. It can knock your trusty shopper's goggles right off your head. It can make you choose the wrong person, make you worry about the wrong things when you're dating, and then it can foul things up later on.

"Now wait just a minute," I hear some voices saying. "Isn't falling in love the pinnacle of human emotion, a wondrous experience admired by poets, talk-show hosts, and brain physiologists? Are you saying people don't really fall in love, or that it isn't a peak experience?"

Good questions. I am certainly not saying that people don't fall in love. They do, all the time; I've done it more than twice. And it *is* a mind-bending, life-disrupting experience, a unique cocktail of emotions including euphoria, desire, jealousy, hilarity, audacity, loss of one's rational faculties—and a tendency to gaze at the moon. But unfortunately this experience comes with a *belief* hooked onto it. In the thick of the trance we hear Cupid's bell-like voice, telling us that the one we have fallen for is a suitable partner for us.

---

2. I see Cupid as a mischievous imp, kind of like Puck in *A Midsummer Night's Dream*, who specializes in creating chemistry between the wrong people. He has one hell of a chemistry set: those arrows of his are tipped with dopamine and norepinephrine.

"This person is the one for you," Cupid says. "Otherwise you wouldn't be feeling this way!" *(No matter that I've injected special chemicals into your brain.)*

But too much of the time, the person *isn't* the one for us. Take a look at people who once fell in love and see how they're doing now. The divorce rate is said to be around 40 percent, and most of those people started their journey by falling in love. Then add all the couples who stay married even though there's nothing much happening, or there's smoldering hostility. They all fell in love too, years ago. If Cupid were trying to create happiness, he would have a very bad batting average. But he isn't, so that's why he's smiling in all his pics.

What did they see that moved them, these souls who are now alienated? What did they see that made them fall in love? Because people don't fall for just *anyone*. We don't. It takes something special to ignite that rocket ship of emotion. There has to be sexual attraction—mutual—which isn't always easy to find. And beyond that, there's a sense that the other person fits some template we have in our head, what we might call mate-flavored beauty. We think we see a kindred soul.

So why, all too often, do we fall in love with the wrong people?[3] Why doesn't the beauty prove out? Why do we miss a soulmate by a country mile?

Here are some of the reasons:

- It's easier to fall for someone you don't really know. That's because the element of the unknown, the sense of gambling, are perfect conduits for the love chemicals. Virtual strangers get

3. Of course, some marriages fail even when the partners are right for each other. I explored reasons for this in *Better Love Next Time,* and I'll go into how to avoid that fate in the last two chapters of this book.

through Cupid's turnstile quicker than anyone. He waves them on with a jaunty smile, a quick stab of his love potion, and a diamond ring, knowing they'll likely to turn out to be incompatible. Think of it this way. The more you understand a person, the more you see that they're only human. But mad love prefers to think of its object as perfect, wondrous . . . divine. *Infatuation thrives on lack of data.*

- Even when we look for the right clues, we don't look for enough of them. The feeling of mutual attraction makes us way too susceptible; a hint of soulmate–ness and we plunge. "You like sushi too? Then we must be meant for each other!" But the house of compatibility has many rooms, and it takes time to explore them.

- Sexual attraction plays a big role, and unfortunately has nothing to do with how much you have in common as people. We can find a person killingly lust-worthy, then get to know them and discover someone we wouldn't even invite to an ear cleaning.

- Sometimes we go for "the whole package," but externals and status don't warm the heart.

- Sometimes we want to make a purchase, any purchase, so badly that we "induce" the feeling of being in love with whoever is available, and once we're in that blissful state, we're able to blind ourselves to the mistake we're half-deliberately making. That's right, I'm saying falling in love isn't always involuntary, doesn't always crash over us like a wave at high tide. Sometimes we run into the water because it suits our plan.

So the answer to this chapter's title question is no. Falling in love doesn't prove you're with the right guy.

But here's the good news: I think we adult humans can actually tell the difference between *deluded love* and *grounded love,* if we try. When you're going crazy over someone because of agenda—you wanted desperately to fall in love (in time for marriage and kids?) and this person happened to come along—I think, down deep, you know it. When you're deeply incompatible with your new amour, I think you know it. If the only way you can be in love with this guy is to keep telling yourself men are aliens, you can read that sign. When you're out on the town dipping tapenade and sipping Pinot, don't sit there thinking, *That's right, men and women speak different languages, so if he doesn't know what the hell I'm talking about, that's fine.* Your heart is trying to tell you something.

And here's another saving grace, and another reason for the trial period. If you spend enough time with a guy and scope each other out, there will be moments when the intoxication subsides and you are temporarily returned to a clear-eyed state. Take advantage of those moments!

Cool your jets, shopper. Get to know someone a bit before you let yourself fall; or if you can't help it, enjoy the dizzy state but remind yourself every morning before brushing your teeth that it's not a basis to make decisions on. Remember:

If you shop for magic, you are likely to find yourself holding an empty top hat with rabbit poop in it.

Better to find someone you could be happy with and then fall in love with *him.* (If you do the choosing and vetting right, you can.) I said earlier that during the trial period, when you narrow your eyes and peer at Mr. Possible, you are trying to see into the future. You're trying to see what you two will be like in twenty years, what there is in common that will last; how much you're going to enjoy each other's company, and how many things you will dream of doing together, even when you're older. The strangest twist: *you're trying to see what this man will look like to you when you're not madly in love anymore.* That early, intoxicating state is at best the training wheels of the real thing, which will turn out to be richer, deeper, and all in all, a better value.

Just to be clear: am I saying don't fall in love? No, I'm not. I would be a surly curmudgeon indeed if I said that. I hope you do fall in love, swooningly. I'm saying, try to see if there's any substance to it, or is it just Cupid's drugs making you foolish? And don't base major decisions (like moving in together or marriage) only on the fact that you are in love. Give yourself the shopper's advantage: use the tools we've discussed to choose carefully; and after you choose, even if you are smitten, go through a real trial run and see if the connection holds up. Falling in love is one of life's best experiences, if you can look back years later and say, "Yes, I fell for the right guy."

While walking along the beach, I saw two people in a clinch. They stood in the surf, she held his head against her neck. Very lovely—it was like they were making a compact, a covenant. I was working on this section and I thought, we do a brave thing when we pledge our love. It's kind of like being high with someone and deciding that you're going to be fast friends forever, after the drug wears off. You have to make a promise stick, somehow make it punch through the spell you're under to the real world that you'll be in later. May you have more than the spell to get you through.

I'll talk in Chapter 33 about part two of Cupid's scam, even sneakier than part one, where he takes a couple who are nicely launched in marriage and have a real chance to go the distance, and talks them out of it.

But for now, let's look past the magic and continue our tour of your potential mate.

28

why the big rush?

why does one party sometimes rush the relationship even when they've agreed not to?

*W*hen I discussed the pacing of a new relationship in Chapter 14, I said:

> back off when you notice you're doing all the work, and draw the other person out of the bushes. Or if he is pushing too hard, ask *him* to back off so you can feel your wings. Don't rush him, and don't let him rush you.

Why do we sometimes do the opposite? Why do we let one person push too hard, even after agreeing not to?

It's often out of fear—on both sides. The over-eager person is afraid if he lets up, really allows the other to think clearly, she'll go away; and the other person is afraid if she slows her man down, cools his jets, he'll lose interest.

This is not sound thinking. If only a forced pace is keeping things going, you are already in trouble. It usually means that something other than tempo is out of whack—something deeper.

A possible culprit: you don't really belong together, and one person senses that. The other person compensates by pushing too hard, and if they are persuasive and charming enough, we get a grand love affair that ends in heartbreak, usually for the person who let themselves be swept along.

This happened to me once. I was living in a house in LA with a group of people, while happily dating a woman, S, who lived across town. A new woman moved into the house, we'll call her J. She was friendly and in my beholder's eyes, gorgeous, and I would chat with her sometimes, but I didn't sense that we had that much in common. I was analytical, verbal, and a worrier; she was athletic, dynamic, and daring. I admired her, but I wouldn't have pursued her. She, however, fixed her sights on me and was visibly upset when I would bring S home and have a drink with her in the front room. Long story short: J came after me with all of her energy and sleek good looks, she let me know how wonderful I was in her eyes, and I bought it, ditched S, and fell hard for J. For a while—a few months, actually—things went well, and I was in love like I'd never been, walking in a brighter world. Then one day the light changed. I could tell that her love was on the wane, and I got a sinking feeling that I had no cards to play, no way to hold her.

I didn't know the reason for my helplessness then, but it's crystal clear to me now: her passion had never really been about me. She had mistaken me for someone she wanted me to be, and had swept us both along. No wonder that deep down I had always felt a sense of danger with her, and a sadness in my bones. I had ignored my inner voice, and as a result I was that much more devastated by the breakup when it came.

The one-sidedness of things had not escaped me, but I had taken it for a *good* thing, some odd gift from destiny. I should have told her, "Listen, you can't just run the show—you're not the director. Back off a bit, I need to have a hand in this too." If I had, maybe we would have realized that we were miles apart.

The other cause of rushing is that you do belong together but it's the wrong time in your lives. The next story is about that.

OFFER ENDS TODAY

Karen met Will accidentally, at a pretzel cart downtown. They hit it off right away and made a date. Karen had recently gotten out of a painful relationship and had her bar set low, hoping just to have a little fun and keep things light. Will was lonely and horny. He had been unattached for a long time and felt his love life needed a kick-start; his career was also stalled but he wasn't up to facing that just now, so he needed a major diversion.

Karen's heart wasn't ready for big risks; Will's heart was craving them.

Ironically (given what was about to unfold), Will possessed exactly the traits that could give Karen what she wanted. He was a natural mimic with a wonderful sense of the absurd, and he brought that out in her, so they were often in laughter to the point of tears. They loved a lot of the same things, from film-and-TV trivia to ethnic food to board games. And they were torrid together in bed. Their mutual music was so good . . .

If only their tempos had matched. Will called Karen every day. He wanted to see her every evening. He knew when she was leaving work and waited for her to get home so he could call her. So Karen felt as if she couldn't dawdle, couldn't maybe go to an art museum or a perfume sale, because she could feel that pressure from Will, that ardent hope that she would be home when he called.

She kept saying yes, and they kept doing whatever Will wanted to do, because he would ask her out before she had time to muster a plan. Once in a while she tried to propose something different, like going to a play or to the arboretum, but Will had a way of dismissing these suggestions, as if to say, "Why do we need distractions when it's so great just to be together?" So Karen went along with him, and nearly every day they ended up at one of the three restaurants he liked or at his place, where they ordered moo shoo and did the nasty. She *always* enjoyed his company. She wasn't sure how deeply she felt about him because she hadn't had a chance to be alone, catch her breath, experience his absence, and feel her heart reach out to him.

About seven days into the relationship, Will started saying "I love you." At first Karen tried to deflect it with a joke or thank him as if it was a compliment. When that proved insufficient she would reply in a put-on stuffy British accent, "Jolly good, I adore you too, old chap." But she felt increasingly cornered; it seemed unkind not to say it back to him, and she didn't wish to be unkind. It made her feel cold, uncaring, lacking a romantic pulse.

The gallant Will took care of that problem by replacing it with a bigger one. At the three-week mark he took Karen to an expensive steak house where champagne and roses awaited, and asked her to marry him. It put her in an agonizing position, because she really liked him and truly needed the good times they were so capable of having together. She felt like a shopper facing a "Sale Ends Today!" sign.

It was too much. She said she'd think it over and the next day she broke off with Will.

That led to an interesting thing. Thrown back on himself, Will woke up.

He chastised himself for rushing Karen and ignoring her state of damage and hesitancy. Without the love affair to distract him, he had to face his real issue—his stalled career in consulting. His unemployment was running out. He had to overcome discouragement and fear, and make a new plan. He needed to build a new client base or find an employer. He tried both and the second one led to a new job in software training. Will gradually recovered from the tailspin he'd been in and saw all too clearly that he'd pressured Karen in order to put a Band-Aid on his own life.

A year later she called him, "just to say hello," and they started seeing each other again. This time he was in no hurry, and she was ready for more. The underlying problem had never been a lack of fit between them: they "got" each other in a host of ways. In fact, Karen's refusal to accept the mismatch in tempos had forced Will to the solution they needed.

29

why does a guy suddenly disappear
when things were going so well?

is it commitment-phobia or something else?

*U*nlike a new chair, a new man may seem to be at home in your world for weeks or months and then disappear. There are really two parts to this puzzle, short-term and longer.

Short-term

You've seen each other a few times and things seemed to go swimmingly, and then the guy suddenly becomes unreachable. You agree to go to an Italian restaurant and he cancels and says let's reschedule. But the rescheduling never happens. He's gone.

Why the brush-off?

There are so many possible explanations that you may never get the answer. There may not *be* one answer. Maybe the guy wasn't really unattached and was just testing the waters. Maybe he was intimidated by your career, or in some way by you. Maybe he felt you weren't his type but didn't feel he could say that. Many people—men *and* women—would rather do almost anything than reject someone to their face. So they lie and say, "Great, let's do that," in order to slip away without being the bad guy. Then later from a safe distance they wriggle out.

It's frustrating not to know exactly what happened, but in every one of these cases he wasn't the right guy for you.

Long-term

This is the more bizarre one. Few things are more confounding than the guy who seems all cozy and attached for months, gets close to your puppy, says and does all the right things, and then suddenly vamooses. Why do guys do this?

There are several reasons, and some of them may surprise you.

He doesn't like your puppy.

A better theory is that he was using you (maybe for sex), was never really into it, and went along for the ride until things got too heavy. That happens, but if you do a good job of vetting him, you are unlikely to be blindsided by it.

No, the cases that are most baffling and make you suspect the dude of multiple-personality disorder are something murkier.

Blinded by the quest. One big factor is this. Sometimes men postpone the question of whether they want something. Instead, they try for it, just to see if they can get it. If you're an interesting woman who is not an easy conquest, a guy may be focused on winning you, not because he is sure he wants you but because he can't resist the challenge.

So first he has to win you. He does everything in his power to make that happen, piling on the royal treatment. And about the time you feel he has proven himself and you are ready to commit, he picks up the signal that you are now in his grasp. For the first time he has an option, so he takes a reading on his emotions. How does it feel to have you in his life, as a done deal? And surprise: with the chase over and a stable situation forming, he may find that the air has gone out of the balloon.

The threat of being known. If he wasn't subjected to much scrutiny up to this point, he may find the situation has turned prickly. Now he is faced, not with an amusing filly to chase, but with a woman who is for real. He is expected to have a relationship, and his actual values and job and personality will be measured by someone who has standards and needs. That is too scary. Suddenly he is exposed, open to evaluation in a whole new way. You've changed in his eyes, from a tantalizing prize to an unwanted test of his worth. When he runs from you, he's running from self-knowledge.

That's not a very worthy motive, but it does underline how important it is to really get to know a guy during the trial period, instead of trying to make things pleasant by keeping it shallow. If that kind of exploration scares him away, he would have run in the end anyway; and if it doesn't, it is very good news: it means he *likes* being known by you.

But there's another kind of motive that can make a man vamoose.

Fear of disaster. A man sometimes sees danger down the line when the woman has an overriding agenda for marriage and kids, and a head full of bridal magazines. He wonders if she is really in love with him, or in love with her plan. He senses the Cupid debacle down the road, where "in love" will end and all bets will be off. So he tries to test love by trying love, to hedge against disaster by looking for compatibility. If he isn't sure he has found it, he turns tail and runs. Safer to keep looking and find a better match.

She prefers not to look at the danger, but she has an answer to it. If, god forbid, she turns out not to really like her husband, she can move on and probably do well in the divorce. He sees a fair chance of being discarded. She whispers to herself, "If all else fails, at least I'll get the kids." While he mutters, "I won't."

When he leaves, it's because the trial period has only now ended for him and it ushered in a negative verdict. Call it commitment-phobia if you want, but he didn't have enough evidence to make such a huge bet—to bet his life. Maybe it was because things went too fast; maybe because she was driving the bus. And maybe because the evidence just wasn't there. He tried it out, right down to the wire, and he wasn't convinced.

I haven't gone into why a guy just vanishes in these situations, instead of explaining himself. There are plenty of reasons, they aren't hard to imagine. There's guilt, there's lack of the self-knowledge that would produce an explanation, there's fear of losing the argument, fear of being the bearer of bad news, and even fear of hurting someone. (Leaving does enough harm; why compound it by giving your *reasons*?) The longer a relationship has gone on and the more splendid it has seemed, the more embarrassing it is to call a halt. This breaking up isn't easy for either gender and these reasons aren't just true of men.

Fortunately, most surprise goodbyes can be avoided by keeping the previous two chapters in mind. Don't fall for Cupid's scam by slipping into deluded love, and don't let either person be the sole driver or rush the other into a false union. Take turns instigating things and both people are more likely to develop a real involvement. Finally, don't assume that by dodging the trial period you can avoid its sting. The real lesson here is that the more enthusiastically you get to know someone, the less likely it is you will be hit by nasty bombshells.

30

should you judge a man by what he is now, or by what he could be?

*N*ews bulletin: Many of us aren't living the lives we were seemingly born for. We haven't had time to get there yet, or we didn't realize right off what we wanted, or we got sidetracked into a situation that is not easy to get out of.

It's hard for overachievers to understand, but not everyone is living in a world where they get to be themselves and prevail. A lot of people are chewed up by society or circumstance or bad luck, and they end up in a damaged state, or at least a suppressed state, not quite firing on all cylinders but still trying to try.

One of the factors that keeps people down is loneliness. I gave that a good workout, for years.

One of the things that lifts them is love.

The greatest gift in the world is to see the true soul shining in another person that's already gone partly false, and love them for that truth, and let it come back out. As my friend D.G. Reid put it, real love calls into being the best in both people.

In a weird way, shopping is a bridge between the person you are now and the person you want to be. So is finding a partner.

We rise to meet the other person. We want to be worthy of them; and we want to live up to their absurdly positive vision of us. They give us a new contract, a new chance to be. And we do that for them.

Can people change? The conventional wisdom says no, but it's all wet.

Judge your partner not by what they are, but by what they could be with your support.

Maybe a soulmate is someone whose highest gifts you can appreciate—and vice versa. And that sometimes takes a while to figure out, as do the gifts themselves. The best developments may not have happened yet. It may take two to make them happen.

I wrote a song called "You Made My Lies Come True." I'm not going to quote it here, but I'll tell the story behind it.

When I met my partner, I told her I was a writer. Never mind that I was sporadically working on two books but had never had anything published. And I said I was a singer-songwriter, a performer. But the truth was, I had stage fright and had never really gotten comfortable in front of an audience.

Pretty pathetic, eh? But she did a crazy thing: she believed me. She read the things I was putting in my books and she enthused over them. She listened to my songs and liked them.

And then, at two crucial junctures, she changed the course of my history.

One night on the way home from a painful gig where I was not being myself, not being any fun, and basically using my onstage patter to give the audience reasons not to like the next song, she told me, "If you can't be positive, stop talking. Just sing."[1]

---

1. A reckless friend had given me a weekly slot at the club, one hour every Thursday night.

How insulting. She didn't seem to understand that there was a solid *reason* for my negativity. I had occasionally had a few good moments performing for people, but I didn't know what caused them to happen, and I wasn't able to repeat them, so I decided they were magic. No amount of effort would help me; either the gods smiled on me or they didn't. That is why I was so pessimistic; because I had put all my chips on magic. Which wasn't under my control, so I was helpless. And I let that attitude spill into the audience.

After she gave me her advice, I was angry and hurt, but I listened to her. The next week I hardly said a word on stage, no sarcastic apologies, no caveats. I went through my material and by the end I was convinced I had done even worse than usual. I wanted to duck into the kitchen and go out the back alley. But I walked through the spectators and three people told me that was the best they'd ever seen me.

I thought, "This is strange. If I just try, it doesn't go too badly. It isn't about magic after all."

For a week I rehearsed hard and I could feel the quality going up. At the next gig I got on stage in a very unusual frame of mind: optimistic. I wasn't afraid of what they would think; I just wanted to give them a good show. I had fun, I got laughs, the songs came to life. In a year or so I got a band together and after that, performing live became one of my favorite things in the world.

She had taught me not to yearn for magic. Try for something different: the possible.

The second intercession came when I got one chapter of my manuscript published in a collection of men's writings. That seemed to lead to a book deal—at last—and then for no good reason, it fell through. I was in despair because I thought I would never come so close again.

At this dark moment in a cold December, my partner pointed out that the chapter had gotten some good notices. Why didn't I thank some of the reviewers? So I did. That led, through the generosity of another writer, to an agent and a deal. And the book I had told her about six years earlier got published.

Life is a work in progress. But I do feel like I'm doing what I was supposed to do, and enjoying it. That's a huge improvement over where I was.

And it happened because someone looked in my eyes and saw who was inside there, trying to get out. And said, I'm for *you*.

Things aren't always sunny for us, of course. And I know I got lucky. But I also know that love has been here before. In the place where couples affirm the best in each other, and call it into being.

31

if you have fights, does that mean it's not going to work out?

*A*ll couples quarrel sometimes, and occasionally it gets pretty hot and heavy. There's a sense of embarrassment because you're supposed to be in love, and it can be stressful and uncomfortable. You *will* have conflicts and you *will* annoy one another. If you haven't yet gotten there, you haven't come down to the ground yet.

I'm not saying you should deliberately cook up a fight. But assuming you're not floating in a mutual dream of niceness, conflict will happen. If you're doing the trial period right, really testing stuff bravely, you'll both be out of your comfort zones some of the time and that can lead to a few tiffs. You're in uncharted territory. You'll make mistakes, you'll take things the wrong way. And you'll be introduced to adjustments you're going to have to make—which is not always fun.

When trouble erupts, approach it naturally and see what unfolds. Later your head will be cooler and you can sift the new data. How you both react to fights, how you resolve them, and how you move on are all crucial indicators of your chances of going the distance. Here are some *positives* to watch for:

- Neither of you enjoys it. If you feel awful when you're alienated, if you basically can't stand it, that's good. On the other hand, if one or both persons seem to relish the rift, that's not so good. In the middle of a fight you can lose your sense that you even like the other person; if this feels like a great place to be—bad news.

- You don't abuse each other or haul out stored material just to hurt each other. Many things, once said, cannot be taken back. You can forever lose the other person's faith that you are their biggest fan. So don't go there.

- You both explain thoroughly what is making you mad, and you both listen. Maybe you learn something.

- After a cooling-off period (often apart), you hasten to apologize to each other, and each person tries to make it their fault. So you get into a reverse competition, trying to convince the other person why they *aren't* wrong.

- You are extremely relieved when things get back to normal.

- You laugh about it later.

If you find that most of these things are true, it's a good sign that the two of you are capable of having non-destructive fights, which leave the edifice of love still standing.

And here's an important problem to look for when things get adversarial.

Phantoms from the past. Many of us bring a different set of standards to our mate than we do to our friends. We know how to get along with our friends, we accept foibles, we tolerate blatant disagreement. And above all, we don't foist on them our issues from the past.

But when love rears its head, we have a tendency to collapse time. Sometimes we have trouble separating the person we're with—who is trying to be our new partner—from various looming characters from our past, including our parents, siblings, and lovers.

So here's the thing to look for. When you're having a fight with your new guy, do you get the disturbing sense that he is talking to someone else who isn't in the room? That some button you've inadvertently pressed has put him right back in a story with his dad or his first girlfriend, back into a state of hurt, anger, bitterness, or fear?

It's good to have a past, and to have faced it and learned from it. It's even good to have some sadness and regrets, hopefully leavened with humor and positive feelings. But it's hard to connect with someone who is still tangled up in unresolved issues and can't see straight when they look at you.

This sort of thing can be hard to catch while a conflict is happening, but when his reaction is way out of proportion to what triggered it, note that as a clue, and reflect on it afterward. If "wrestling with phantoms" emerges as a pattern, you've got a serious red flag on your hands. If it *sometimes* happens and he is able to identify it, apologize for it, get his perspective back, and be less likely to go there again, that may be a growing pain that you both can live with.

Of course, you aren't immune to this kind of haunting either—no one is. There are hurts from our childhoods and our early loves that never completely go away. So forgive a little and be forgiven.

Summing up, your first few fights are nothing to be dismayed by. They are solid gold. They are a window into that future we talked about, when you'll have to get along without Cupid's potions.

I have two more chapters and I'll bid you farewell. The first concerns when it's time to stop shopping; the second is about long-term satisfaction, and the number one secret of lasting couples.

32

shopping addiction and getting exclusive

I said earlier that the trial period is a sort of audition for a relationship. The twist is that if the audition goes well and you succeed as a couple, the audition becomes part of the play—it turns out to have been its opening act. You don't know whether the time you're spending together is a trial run that will prove unsuccessful, or the first phase of a fabulous long-term relationship. (How's that for a tricky path to walk?)

That's why this section is partly a manual on the first hundred days (or so). If you end up staying with the guy, this is about how to get there.

There are several milestones on the road to commitment. They include starting to sleep together, agreeing to be exclusive, using the L-word, and moving in together. They can happen in different orders for different couples.

They're all important, but right now I want to talk about that crucial decision to be exclusive—to stop seeing other people. Sometimes it is tacit and sometimes it's talked about openly. It means you're really going to give this thing a chance, by giving each other your full romantic attention. What interests me here is that in recent times this step has become much more fraught.

Dating has become shopping, and old shopping habits die hard.

After shopping till we drop, some of us like to comparison shop till we forget what we already bought. Especially online, it's easy to keep your personal ads current and keep browsing those gleaming faces. Men do it too. How does anybody stop long enough to appreciate the partner they've chosen? Can you really value a new person when you're still on the lookout?

The paradox of online dating is that its purpose is to get to a place where you are *not* online dating. But even after you've found a worthy partner, the habit is hard to kick. The constant stimulation of new people wanting to get it on with you is very addictive. Also leading us into temptation are social networking, texting, and tweeting; laptops, smartphones, iPads—and it doesn't stop. All of these brilliant inventions expose us to a deluge of interaction with more people than we used to interact with, and with their friends, and the friends of their friends, or with "everyone." To think that this does not enable a lot of flirting—and a lot of window-shopping (or Windows-shopping)—would be naive.

Which also makes it too easy to jump ship. The new social technologies have created a hair-trigger eject mechanism for whenever you encounter any difficulties in your new relationship. So you never find out the rewards of sticking with it that people used to discover because they had no choice.

Bottom line: our dating culture hasn't caught up with the changes wrought by technology. The boundaries haven't been formulated for what it means to be exclusive. Does anyone know exactly what constitutes cheating anymore—or fidelity?

Is it cheating if he sends sexy text messages to another woman?

Is it cheating if you friend your ex on Facebook?[1]

When you meet your new love at the café, does he hurriedly close his laptop or stop texting on his cell? Do you?

This is serious business. You have to try commitment to test it. You can't have one foot in the boat and one foot out of it, or you won't be able to see where it can carry you. If you think your lover is still checking out other women, still flirting and leaving himself open to invitations, you can't find out what it would feel like to have his heart.

The good news is, there's a gift that a couple can give each other, a mutual offering that can bring you closer and give you a chance to develop trust and intimacy. Here's what to do. When you decide you want to be more exclusive, sit down and talk over what that means to you, how you translate it into our ultra-connected world. (You can't get mad over behavior if you haven't discussed and agreed on whether it's okay.) For example, you may negotiate a cessation of flirting/sexting with third parties, agree to "ratchet it back to platonic" with other people. That means not trolling for new lovers, which includes taking down your profile on dating sites.

HOW TODAY'S TOYS MAKE PEOPLE NEGLECT THE PRIZE THEY SHOPPED FOR

While we're on the subject of technology, here's a point about the long term: For a love to last, two people have to pay attention to each other.

---

1. *Glamour* magazine asked me to comment on four such situations for an article on "What Counts as Cheating Now" (June 2009). My take on the sexting is basically yes, it's cheating; on the friending of an ex, it depends. There can be lots of reasons for talking to an ex, many of them innocent.

But we live in a barrage of information. We consume endless hours exchanging emails that weren't even possible a few decades ago. We have Facebook and texting and IMing and tweeting. Then we have TV and TiVo and video games and the screens just go on and on. Our computers have so many open windows that we don't remember what we were thinking about ten minutes ago. Many people have a TV in every room and a computer for every member of the household. People talking on cell phones drive home from work, and after they walk in the door texting, they get hijacked by more screens.

It's a topsy-turvy priority that makes us think our partners are somehow intruding on more important things, when all they want is for us to look up and listen.

Technology also presents an easy way out, a flat-panel "togetherness." When you're already somewhat distant from your spouse because nothing has happened today to bring you together, it's easier to fall back on passive entertainment that you at least share. But that isn't the same as having a real conversation, and it doesn't help build the bridge between the two of you that needs to be constantly renewed.

Those not busy staying close are busy becoming strangers.

So learn how to be truly together when you and he are together. Turn off your cell phones and BlackBerrys. (Off doesn't mean vibrate; it means leave a message and I'll listen to it later.) We are addicted to interruption these days, hooked on distraction. Do your lover a favor and be with him—if you're not a heart surgeon on call.

33

how Cupid tries to cheat you out of happiness with Mr. Right

and how to beat him at his own game

After a few attempts, you find a great guy, come through the trial period with flying colors, and make a commitment to each other. You're on your way; all systems are go. Will you find long-term satisfaction?

Cupid may give you a pass for a few years, but down the line he has one more trick to play, and in this chapter I want to discuss how to beat him at that game. I talked earlier about the first part of his scam, where he tries to tell you that if you're in love with somebody, you don't need any further proof that you belong together for life. (And he tries to make you fall for people you hardly know, who often turn out to be the wrong ones.)

You got past that unscathed: you gave your heart to a kindred spirit.

But if he can't get you coming, he'll get you going.

Remember that myth of his—the one that says you marry your sweetheart and the two of you have perfect bliss forever after, basting in adoration and mind-boggling sex, always madly in love? It has a new role to play down the line: he uses it to talk you out of staying together.

Here is what happens to many couples.

A few years go by and as we say, the honeymoon is over. They don't feel like they're in love anymore, not so much of the time anyway. They aren't having constant sex. They have some problems. Sometimes they don't get along. They don't even like each other at times.

Oh my: they aren't living up to the benchmark they bought into at the start and still believe in. It brings on a sense of shame, of inadequacy.

So they decide they're not okay, because they've lost the magic, and they break up. And they both find new people, and try to achieve that higher, dreamy level they were told about. The result? They end up leading shallow lives and never rejoining the story that was in progress, the one where a deeper bond was on its way, that *could* have gone on forever, even unto death.

In this sad dismissal, some very significant facts get neglected. They're a pretty good team, after all. They are pretty good co-parents. They know each other better than anyone else does. And they still enjoy each other, and lust after each other, or they would if the embarrassment of not being "in love" wasn't a stifling mantle over them.

That's the problem. But there's a solution.

The secret of couples who last

No one tells our failing lovers the best-kept secret of successful couples who go the distance. What is that secret? It's knowing that romantic love is a game nobody can win. If you (a couple) try to scale the impossible peak of perfect, forever fairy-tale love, you'll end up frozen in a snow drift, but if you beg off from that, you may just end up with something better.

What do enduring couples know? They know that Cupid's promise is a crock. It ain't *like* that in the real world of marriage. The mad infatuation fades and, for those who last and are decently well matched, is replaced. By something less selfish and less shallow. Where we don't always know the way forward, but we learn it by sticking around long enough for it to reveal itself. In the early days of infatuation, our excitement is sparked by our *lack* of knowledge of each other. But later on we bring a greater gift, which can only be given by one who knows another deeply and well. Real marriage is not a picnic in a field of daisies. It isn't a shampoo commercial, or a Viagra commercial. It's about a state that is more real, that is gritty yet noble.

Love.

A burden lifted

There's a kind of emperor's-new-clothes thing going on, where established couples pretend to feel the way Hallmark says they should, but secretly, or not so secretly, they know better. They know how it really feels to live with someone for years, to face their otherness and their conflicting agenda, their flaws and their foibles, to work it out and make it work, to hate them sometimes and fear them sometimes and wish you could be with someone else sometimes, but damn it, in the end you care about them the way you do about your kids or your parents, and it's sexy sometimes, but a lot of the time it isn't, and once in a while, yes, it's romantic. Real couples know that what they're actually living is not the script they were sold. But too often they aren't comfortable with that fact.

To say this may be a splash of cold water. But that can be a salutary thing. Many normal couples have so much going for them. And they need to be given permission to be glad, instead of always feeling somehow wanting. They need the Cupid burden lifted; they need a chance to say, with a sigh of relief, "Thank god, we can stop trying (or faking) this impossible thing, stop trying to meet this impossible standard."

Cupid says, "True love is all that matters." And then he pulls his most insidious move: "If that moonstruck feeling doesn't last, *then it wasn't real in the first place.* You weren't really in love. So why bother nurturing the lower assets you possess?" So two people who are distracted by the romantic dream they're supposed to be living, fail to pay enough attention to two things they actually have. Friendship and sex. They don't take care of their friendship; they treat each other worse than they treat their friends. They don't bother to be sexy, the way they would if they were single and having a torrid romance.

But here is the good news: when you realize what you *really* have, you suddenly know how to go about it. Magic is a hard thing to maintain: no one knows where it comes from, why it leaves, or how to get it back. But friendship and sex are manageable goals. *You know how to be a good friend. You know how to be sexy.* So don't be seduced into thinking that the fact that you once fell in love somehow gives the two of you an excuse to fall down in these areas, to neglect each other. It's so easy to marginalize one's mate and put them at the end of the line—as if their "true love" status means they don't need your attention at the diner, or your charm in the evening. It isn't right to punish them for not living up to the fairy tale: no one can.

As I've said before, falling in love is a wonderful thing, if you do it with the right person. If not, it can lead to a mighty fall. And I think your best protection is taking the time to really get to know someone, as I've recommended in the trial period. If they turn out to be a great match for you, you can cherish the early infatuation forever. Even as you evolve beyond it.

Falling in love pulls time together and makes it seem as if a continuous run of hours and days are all transmuted by a dizzying alchemy—into an eternal, dreamlike present. But marriage is different, after the honeymoon. Marriage is a series of discrete experiences, some neutral, some joyous, some annoying, some harrowing, some boring, some funny. For that reason it is impossible for marriage to seem to us to be the same thing that made us sign on. Yet at its best, marriage forges its own time signature, one with a past and a future, rich with purpose and regret and gratitude, and the sense of having stayed the course and helped someone else believe that human beings are made of true stuff.

Wherever it came from, the myth of perfect bliss is past its expiration date. The smart shopper will take it with a grain of salt, and resolve to make do with real, adult love.

acknowledgments

$\mathscr{I}$want to thank my sister Kathrine, the first serious shopper that I knew (as related in the Introduction), and surely a champion of that species. She walked just ahead of me through the formative years and let me scope out each new wind before it hit me. As college students, we sat in Yorkville over cafés au lait and European pastries and forged a frank connection, less like siblings than like two rookie therapists cutting their teeth on each other. She has always given me an open window on her experience of life.

My sister Ann never subjected me to the rigors of shopping, but brought out a whole different spectrum of feelings in me because we were far enough apart in age never to be competitive with each other. Her openheartedness, perceptiveness, and passion have kept this prodigal older brother from slipping out of orbit and educated me in ways I constantly rely on.

It is not good to leave out a sibling and I will thank my brother Geoffrey when I write a book about fishing for thoughts instead of fish, laughing until you cry, and the comfort of not being the only son.

I thank Roberta Parigini who was the second great shopper that I knew, who lifted my sights to the kind of shirt that a man can care about, and whose droll humor, scary intelligence, courage, and knowledge of northern Italian cuisine carried me and her through hell and heaven.

Then I want to mention my oldest male friend in the world, Donald Reid. I was fortunate to stumble on such a pal in early childhood. While operating as junior detectives and winning occasional canoe races, Don and I worked through many riddles of life together and we continue to do so today. During the conception of this book he jogged me with new perspectives, calls to action, and brilliant ripostes that showed me how rich this topic is. He also improved my understanding of the use of "that" and "which."

I thank Debra Donahue who is my heart's companion on the never-predictable road. She loves to shop for other people more than for herself, and she sees in them more than they do. Her complicated heart and fine-grained mind show me a benchmark that I should be so lucky as to aspire to. Before, during, and after the writing of this book she has been her usual fertile source of ideas, insights, stories, humor, encouragement, and corrective advice. There's no way this book exists without her.

I want to thank Julie McElroy, Rich Mayone, and Patti Goyette for their astute feedback on relationships and their love of seafood. I am grateful to Jackie and Trace Brown for sharing their unconventional journey on an old hotel porch.

I thank Marni Jackson for providing a writer's shoulder to cry on and a writer's ear to vent to, and for her generous, persistent friendship, which has benefited me in so many ways.

I want to thank Leah Fairbank, recently of John Wiley & Sons Canada, for pulling this project out of me and believing in it, and me, for a third time. There is no way to summarize what I owe her as an editor, ally, and friend. I deeply thank publisher Jennifer Smith for her crucial support from the beginning. Publicity manager Erin Kelly has been a charge of positive energy all along, as she conducted me into a strange new world of radio and TV and steered me past February storms across Canada. I thank managing editor Alison Maclean for the cool, witty way she picked up a project in midstream and saw that no threads got dropped. Production Editor Pauline Ricablanca brought the final revisions in for a flawless three-point landing, while finding time to mentor this pdf parachutist. Everyone at Wiley has been unstintingly gracious and good to me for four years now, in spite of my excitable and sometimes contrary nature.

I thank Judy Phillips for completing an arduous, two-tiered editing job in grand style and making many improvements to this book. Any errors that remain are only signs of my perversity.

Finally I want to thank Sam Hiyate of The Rights Factory. If he keeps on in the same way, he's in danger of giving agents a reputation for accessibility, loyalty, and kindness that will not make their jobs any easier.

This book was written in Cape May, New Jersey, and I am grateful for having landed here by the sea and for the people who make this town feel like home.